TARA'S CROSS
The Magnificent Sighting

G. J. Bachmann

iUniverse, Inc.
New York Bloomington

iUniverse books may be ordered through booksellers or by contacting:

iUniverse
1663 Liberty Drive
Bloomington, IN 47403
www.iuniverse.com
1-800-Authors (1-800-288-4677)

ISBN: 978-1-4401-4472-1 (pbk)
ISBN: 978-1-4401-4471-4 (ebk)

Printed in the United States of America

iUniverse rev. date: 10/13/2009

I have sought to protect living persons by changing certain names and, when
necessary, altering character descriptions and events. The dialogues in this book are
constructed from clear memories of their content, and with an ear for the nuances.

To mother and child. This good world of ours is held together by the heroic angels of our dreams.

The Holy Father looks fit and is headed for Yankee Stadium.
Pope Benedict XVI has blessed Ground Zero. Now is the
time for healing for 9/11 families and survivors.

The Holy Father smiled when he saw the cover of the advanced copy of *Tara's Cross*.
Retired Firefighter George Bachmann Ladder 10 at
Ground Zero on Papal visit April 20, 2008.

PREFACE

I soldiered on after September 11, 2001 as best I could, but in my heart and gut I knew I had a story to tell. I kept close to my family, my word processor, and my therapy to heal my mind and body. I even took in a writing course. I made a science out of reading other September 11 survival stories, and realized I too had a calling. My plot was simple. I opened up on the recall of the emotionally charged fifth anniversary, flashing back to my early days of physical and mental therapy, and recuperation; following through with the events that happened to me that day, the aftermath, and redemption that followed. I had a hundred-page accountability of what happened to me on September 11, but it was only after I added the material from my therapeutic dream journal, I was asked to keep by my 9/11 grief counselor and physician, did the story of *Tara's Cross* start to unfold. I teeter-tottered on the fence of indecision regarding whether to release my memoir as a book. The months and years went by. Finally one day I heard New York City Fire Department's Chief of Department Salvatore Cassano being interviewed on television. In his interview at the finish line of the Firefighter Steven Siller Tunnel to Towers Memorial Run which is held annually, he said "Not all 9/11 stories have surfaced yet." I went back to chasing my dream. I have maintained since 2002, written articles and essays, exclusively on the subject, and have testified under oath about the circumstances surrounding the two highest ranking chiefs. I believe this to be true.

I'm grateful every day to still be here for my family, and to write about the heroes I served with on September 11, 2001.

Contents

Dreaming, Waking, and Recalling the Fifth Anniversary of 9/11

In these few hours, in the hours before dawn, I walk these restless dreams alone. As I fall through the web of the dream catcher I realize that if I should die before I wake, that in dreams no pain will kiss my brow. At other times, I can't feel my feet touch the ground. Always, these dreams echo on themselves—always the same and always a little different.

That day recurs in every dream. That day, those of us who survived cried a cry so hard and deep that we thought our hearts would never mend. Tonight, once more in sleep's embrace, I'm going deep.

I know why this dream recurs: The fifth anniversary of 9/11 has me on the ropes. The tension and electricity of the brain twists memories into another survivor's dream. It crystallizes, shatters, and is caught into the winds of Morpheus, the god of sleep.

Off I go. I'm floating in midair in full New York City Fire Department combat gear, black fire-retardant Nomax with bright yellow neon reflection stripes, helmet, bunker jacket, pants, boots, and gloves. It's night and I'm about fifteen feet up in the air in the middle of Broadway in lower Manhattan. The city below is desolate; there are no people or vehicles. I descend toward the pulverized ash-coated pavement below.

I'm alone on my knees on the sidewalk, holding on to the iron gates of St. Paul's Chapel. Through them I see the fluted columns and I feel a cold, piercing wind turn the corner on Vesey Street. It rattles and ruffles the mimeograph papers and handmade leaflets by the loved ones and family members of the Honored Dead. Holding on to the gates, I pull myself to my feet and head toward Vesey. I turn the corner and pass the old headstones in the graveyard beyond St. Paul's. I notice that my boots aren't touching the ground anymore. I'm airborne again, ascending over the fiery ruins and devastation of what was once the World Trade Center. I float by the unimaginable carnage and fire. Twisted girders lay like pickup sticks in the shadow of precariously upright, smoldering debris-covered façade. To my left, I see my wounded firehouse, the only one to sustain structural damage because of the attack. Fire laps from every window of buildings around the wreckage's perimeter. It's a perfect man-made hell. Madness, madness!

I finally touch down on West Street between Vesey and Liberty Street. A swirl of ash kicks up as my boots hit the ground. I know where I am now, and I know why I'm here. I reach down into my turnout jacket pocket to find my little red flashlight and slowly start out for the North Tower ruins. It's still dark out. The radiant heat hits me like an invisible wall. I snap down the visor on my fire helmet to protect my face and move in. I crouch down low in a prone position and move forward under a cluster of girders and debris. *Tonight, I'm gonna find them,* I tell myself. *Tonight, I'm going deep. I've got to find them and thank them—to tell them to their heroic faces, "We have not forgotten!"*

I wake up staring at the bedroom ceiling in our Brooklyn brownstone, next to my wife and our child. It all makes sense now as morning light shines through the stained glass window and I hear the birds chirping in the backyard. Just dreaming again. But today is September 11, 2006, the fifth anniversary. I roll over and kiss my apple-headed miracle baby, my Tara. Her name is Gaelic for "Tower." She must have snuck into bed with us last night. Soon, her mother will wake her, give her breakfast, and dress her. I'll shower, shave, and put on my uniform. We'll both kiss her mother good-bye, and I'll deliver the little princess to school. Tara was just a couple of weeks old when her mother, while holding her in her arms, had watched the towers fall on television, knowing that my firehouse was directly across the street.

Today, I'll jump on the R train and head down to the Ground Zero ceremonies. Standing in uniform at the formation for the Ten House, my fire station, a formation which is no easy task for a survivor. There's really not much in the way of visuals: There's a high, clear gate surrounding a sixteen-square-acre canyon with a couple of posters on the gate giving some history about Engine 10 and Ladder 10. (A small museum has since been built to the right of the firehouse, and a bronze frieze—a sculpted wall—has been mounted around the left corner on the exterior of the firehouse, depicting the heroism of the many. The construction is ongoing.)

The firefighters and officers of Engine 10 and Ladder 10, along with a handful of survivors from that fateful Tuesday morning, stand at attention. We salute no fewer than four times, as well as listen to the names of the honored dead, being announced by family members and friends. The four salutes represent the two times that planes struck the towers, then the collapse of both the South and North towers. Anyone standing in the formation without a good pair of dark sunglasses is a damned fool unless you don't care if everyone sees you cry. I've often felt throughout the years that the calling of names by the family members and loved ones is like a direct line to heaven.

"Mother, we love you and miss you," a child might say.

"Daddy, you are in our hearts wherever we go," a teenager reveals.

Multiply that by about three thousand, and it's understandable why the average participant may be reduced to grappling with their rawest human emotions and forced to remove their "camouflage," dark glasses, because of the rivers of tears that flow from their eyes. Even the hardest and saltiest of firefighters, by the end of the day, would beg for a beverage—for medicinal purposes, of course!

The Bronze Sculpted Exterior Wall to 10 House at Ground Zero

They say there's a good chance of a presidential visit. President Bush is in town. The fifth anniversary at Ground Zero also plays host to Britain's Fire Brigades, and a few of the female English firefighters have the cutest accents. The handshakes and goodwill from brother firefighters and officers is a positive sign for me of this event. The warm reception from the captain of the house, Captain Engel, makes me feel as if I still belong, when I know that I'm just your average retired fireman. As we make our annual pilgrimage to this Hallowed Ground and pay tribute to those killed by the terrorist attack of September 11, 2001, I can't help but feel that somehow I am a little special. Not only because against all odds, I survived, which every day I thank God on my knees for, but being I was privy to an unknown piece of history, a historical secret that lay dormant inside me during the early weeks and months after 9/11. This historical secret drove me to the brink.

It wasn't until after my recovery that I was finally able to write about it. My story has neither changed, nor faltered. In addition to testifying to it under oath before the members of the 9/11 Commission, I wrote articles and essays and finally recorded the entire story at the national StoryCorps Project's special booth, set up on the Tribute site, near the PATH trains right on the other side of Ground Zero. David Isay, the founder of StoryCorps, picked up my story and invited me to the grand opening of the booths. Then, he sent the whole thing to the Archives of the Library of Congress in Washington D.C.

The point is I have lived with this story a long time. As I stand blurry-eyed from the emotion-packed day in front of Ten House, I easily recall the "Magnificent Sighting on West Street" and flash back to a time of monumental distress for myself and my little family.

Voices tell tales of 9/11

BY ADAM LISBERG
DAILY NEWS STAFF WRITER

MIKE ALBANS DAILY NEWS

A booth that plays voice recordings by 9/11 survivors and family members of victims opened yesterday at the PATH station at Ground Zero.

A MEMORIAL MADE of sound opened its doors at Ground Zero yesterday, using the voices of those who survived 9/11 to honor those who perished.

The StoryCorps booth in the World Trade Center PATH station will allow survivors, rescuers and victims' families to record 40-minute interviews of what they saw, whom they lost and how they remember.

Those interviews will be archived with the Library of Congress and likely will become part of the permanent museum of the World Trade Center attacks — but they are also deeply gratifying for the people who get interviewed.

"It helped me purge a lot of what's going on," said George Bachmann, a firefighter who broke his back on 9/11 and recorded an interview about it. "In order to heal, you have to hear the story."

David Isay, a longtime radio documentary producer and oral historian, founded StoryCorps in 2003 as a way to capture Americans talking about their lives.

The project has recorded 3,000 stories across the range of American life, with a goal of recording 250,000 in the next 10 years.

"Part of what's so important is remembering who these people were when they were alive, before Sept. 11," Isay told family members who gathered for the opening yesterday. "I give you my word that your loved ones will never, ever be forgotten."

alisberg@nydailynews.com

CHAPTER 1

Was There Some Kind of Collapse or Something?

All was peaceful in Brooklyn. Daddy was home from the hospital. I knew I didn't make a pretty picture, trussed up like some Frankenstein monster with bandages around my head and neck and casts on my body. But as I looked around our second-floor bedroom, I felt, for the moment, that all was well. I was home with Annie, my wife of fifteen years, and our baby daughter, Tara, in the three-story brownstone in Brooklyn's Park Slope, a neighborhood of similar homes, where the stoop with its tall steps stands side by side with the stoops of other brownstones. I was in one of the coziest neighborhoods in one of our country's biggest cities. I might not have had the clearest picture of what exactly was going on, and I knew I had looked better, but I was breathing and I was home with my family.

When I think back, I probably looked like a doubled-over, balloon-headed freak. The diagnosis was complicated: burns around the neck, face, and head areas; severe head and neck trauma; and my back had

1

been broken in two places. The doctors had to monitor my head—the right side of my cranial region was distended about a half-inch. My right eye was questionable; only time would tell if everything would heal.

But in a way, I was able to avoid the fear and anxiety that such a diagnosis might produce. As you see I had absolutely no recollection of how I'd come by these injuries and only a fuzzy idea of how bad they were. I knew I was injured. The bandages and braces told me that, as did the constant throbbing headache behind my leaking right eye. My body was wrapped with huge elastic Ace bandages, and my burns were covered with ointment. But notwithstanding the reality before me, I still couldn't remember what the hell had happened to me. I was suffering from what is known as short-term retrograde amnesia. That was the fancy name; all I knew was that something had hit me—hit me hard, and all I could draw was a blank.

What I didn't know at the time was that I, a firefighter with Ladder 10/Engine 10, had been rescued from beneath the rubble of the Twin Towers, those massive buildings that had shadowed Ten House and made up a large part of our response area. I'd been found under the North Tower on West Street, deep from within the epicenter of what would come to be known as Quadrant 1. I'd survived somehow although my memory had been temporarily left there. A couple of weeks or a couple of months down the line, the conflict—the pressure to remember—would surface. But when I came home from the hospital, I was in a healing mode, quite unaware of the cause of my injuries.

Not that I made a good patient. I'm fifty-five now as I write this. Even before becoming a New York City firefighter, I had an active life, served in Vietnam, and saw action there. I'm not the sort to lie in bed. And so after sleeping for two straight days and lying in bed for five, I wanted out. As soon as I could manage it, I hobbled down the brownstone stairs to our living room. Due to all of the bandages and my limp, I had to walk backward down the stairs. With one hand on the wooden banister and my cane in the other, I hopped step by step ever so slowly. The frustration was the worst part.

"Annie, Annie," I yelled for my wife halfway down and couldn't stand it anymore. "Could you give me a hand before I kill myself?"

"Daddy, what are you doing out of bed?"

She stood at the base of the staircase and stared up at me. Her sweet face was at odds with her stern nurse's tone. Annie and I "Mommy" and "Daddy" each other pretty constantly since little Tara joined our family, completing it and putting our hearts at rest. But right then, I wasn't in the mood. I was uncomfortable, awkward, and confused.

"Who the hell put this girdle on me?" I asked, lowering my voice because our daughter—our little miracle—might hear me. Barely three months old, Tara was too young to understand my language, but I knew she could pick up on my tone.

"It's an orthopedic girdle," Annie answered as she climbed up the steps to help me and, I suspected, to keep me from fussing at the stretchy bandages around my waist. "Leave it on, Daddy."

Despite her playful tone, I could tell she was putting on her nurse mode and about to order me back to bed.

"It's itching the hell out of me, Irish," I retorted back with my nickname for her, a tribute to her blond curls, sparkling eyes, and to her proud Old World heritage.

This time, she heard the stress in my plea. In response, she placed her arms around me before her practical side kicked back in.

"I have some anti-itch lotion in the cabinet downstairs," she whispered, agreeing to help me down to the kitchen.

For perhaps the first time, I realized that I was lucky to not only be married to an emergency room nurse, but to one of the senior nurses of the Fire Department's Medical Division. She understands burns and isn't afraid of injuries, and I'd never been so grateful. There was one more thing to be thankful for.

"The baby is still sleeping," she told me. "I have the monitor turned on."

With my sweet Annie's help, I got me the rest of the way down the central staircase and seated in a kitchen chair. She applied the anti-itch ointment where she could reach to apply it under my bandages, and that helped me settle down.

Once I was no longer itching, my body reminded me that I'd been asleep for some forty-eight hours. I was famished, and so Annie gave me tea and some Irish oatmeal following up with chicken soup and saltines, all of the time smiling and giving me the eye with those big blues her mother and father gave her forty-odd years ago. Although we had lived in this cozy brownstone for more than ten years, everything in the kitchen looked new to me. The knickknacks, spice racks, dishes, and porcelain cups sent over from Ireland by the Boland clan of Mayo were things of beauty and wonder. I felt a sense of comfort as if I'd never seen them before and they hadn't been there every morning for our ten years here, and calm came over me. We listened to the baby moving on the monitor and said nothing for a while. Perhaps we were just catching our breath from our struggle down the stairs, but it was a lovely quiet, coming from a peaceful place deep within. It allowed me to remember some of the good times.

I'd fallen in love with a blond-haired nurse, Anne-Marie Tobin, the daughter of Bridget Boland and Thomas Tobin, in the late 1980s. I'd courted her as best I could on a fireman's pay, taking her for walks through Brooklyn's own urban oasis, Prospect Park. Every payday we'd go out for dinner to the Park House, on the park circle at Brooklyn's Windsor Terrace. We shared so much that the lack of serious funding didn't matter. During our walks around our neighborhood or over a good steak, we talked for hours. We'd both been on the job for a while by then, and we found ourselves bonding over our dedication to civil service, our love for our work, and perhaps most of all, our devotion to the wonderful city we served.

We did not share everything though. My family hails from Germany, and Annie's is 100 percent Irish. We both take pride in our families and how they've made their way in this country, but everyone is Irish on St. Patrick's Day, particularly the firefighters. And so every St. Patrick's Day, we'd both join the march in the city—Annie with the nurses and I with my fellow firefighters, and we'd meet at the Armory after the parade. We were a noticeable couple—me in uniform and Annie, the Fire Department nurse, with her bright eyes and golden curls. Maybe we were even a bit of a cliché, but we loved it when high-ranking Fire Department officers and politicians would tease, "So when are the fireman and the nurse gonna hook up?"

The when came in November 1991. The ceremony was pure New York City Fire Department. Members of Squad 1 formed an honor guard, Fire Department–style, raising the halligans and hooks over our heads. Even those not familiar with firefighter's terminology may recognize the halligan, the hooked crowbar-like tool designed to get us into buildings and out of scrapes. But this time the halligans and hooks hailed our way into matrimony. Annie was in flowing white satin with a garland holding her veil back from her golden bangs; I was in white tie and tails. We exited the church in Park Slope under a canopy of halligans, greeting the world for the first time as Mr. and Mrs. Bachmann. The knot was tied in a bowline on the bight; Bridie Boland's daughter had me in one of the world's most secure knots.

Annie and George Bachmann at the Armory after
St. Patrick's Day Parade 1997

I was lost in the memories, those pleasant days long past. The silence was broken finally by the sound of Tara rolling over.

"So, Irish," I asked Annie, "Did we get the number of the truck that hit me?"

"George! Remember what you promised the doctor," she snapped back. "We wouldn't discuss it until you were feeling a little better."

I was teasing her, of course, but already the blankness had begun to bother me. *How did I get this way? What had happened?* There were no clues left for me. On the doctor's advice, Annie had rid the house of newspapers and even disconnected the television, but it is hard to shut out the world entirely.

Just as I finished eating, Tara began to cry, her small but sturdy wail coming through loud and clear over the monitor. Annie started upstairs to the baby's room, leaving me alone to fend for myself.

"Baby Tara, Baby Tara, is someone hungry?" Over the monitor I heard the sweet sounds of a mother talking to her baby in the gentlest voice.

What I didn't know was that with my asking questions, her stress level had started to rise, too. She later told me that she thought, "My God, how will I tell him? How will I break it to him? About the men who are unaccounted for and still missing? How will I tell him about Captain Patty Brown or Father Judge who had once counseled him?"

She later told me everything about that night and how she decided to try to delay breaking the news. She thought I needed more time to heal. She brought the baby downstairs, but they only got as far as the landing before Annie's plan shattered. I watched as her face changed for a moment and she held the baby without saying a word. I could tell something bothered her. But before I could decipher what it all meant, my thoughts were interrupted by something on the radio…

Somehow, using my cane and my one good leg, I got out of the kitchen chair. I was leaning against the wall at the bottom step with my cane in my hand. I looked up to her, holding the baby at the top of the landing.

"Annie," I asked, "I heard Mayor Giuliani on the radio. Was there some kind of a big collapse or something?"

My question caused her to freeze and her eyes drifted toward the radio, which she had left on. I noticed her color drain and her eyes glaze over as though she was overwhelmed and wishing for a simpler time. The moment was broken by Tara's cry. I stared at her in utter confusion until I felt something trickle down the side of my face. I saw her eyes blink, and she came back into the moment. She cuddled our crying daughter and came to my side with a gentle touch. There was something in her touch that seemed to say even though she has something weighing on her, she still has us to hold on to.

Chapter 2

The Crying Doctor

Dr. Mahoney's office could have been any doctor's office in Brooklyn. Five steps up from the street in one of the homey brick brownstones that fill our borough. The office door opened onto a small official-looking waiting room, which in addition to seating provided magazines from months and even years past. Most visitors went right from there into a little examining room with its table, a row of canisters and equipment, and the constant smell of rubbing alcohol. And then they went into the office, a consulting room, with a desk, where the small, stern man talked to his patients.

That was where Dr. Mahoney differed from his colleagues. Although his office had that same professional look—a big desk, a couple of old leather-backed chairs, and a window looking out over Park Slope—his office had something else. In place of citations, awards from various professional groups, or notices listing his qualifications as a specialist or a member of whatever brotherhood, Dr. Mahoney's office walls were covered with photos.

That was the first thing any visitor notices. The photos—snapshots, really—dozens of them depicted the good doctor in all the different phases of his career and with all his varied friends and colleagues. There he was accepting awards from different Fire Commissioners. There he was shaking hands with high-ranking political officials, with friends, and at various social events. Although the prestigious sheepskin diploma that confirmed Kevin Mahoney, MD, as a licensed physician looked impressive centered on the wall, the pictures were most remarkable: Kevin Mahoney, MD, sure, but Kevin Mahoney was a person with his extensive family, friends, acquaintances, and colleagues collected from his full duty-devoted life.

Dr. Mahoney was a small man, but his thick glasses gave him a certain gravity and authority, like the school principal you used to be afraid of or the teacher you would never cross. Dr. Mahoney also never—I mean *never*—smiled, and that compounded your first impression of him. But it had been different; he had been a different man. The photos showed a happier man with his buddies and about to start a friendly foot race.

Annie knew this other side of Dr. Mahoney because she had worked with him for several years at the Fire Department's Medical Division before he had left for private practice. She'd been his colleague before he opened up his own office a block away from our house. She'd grown to trust him as a consummate professional. That long relationship, that memory of better times, was the main reason she'd called him. And why, when she asked him if he would examine my head injuries, he quickly gave us an appointment.

Despite all his photos and evidence of human contact, he was extremely lonely the morning we went to see him. Although he was too professional to mention it, close up shop, and take time off, the truth was that he—like much of the city—was in mourning. For him, our national trauma had been personal. The short, stern man who sat at that tidy desk had lost three close friends at Cantor Fitzgerald, as well as many other good friends from the Fire Department when the towers fell. He had confided and shared with Annie during intense conversations his experiences that day, and she had relayed that day of horror to me.

He'd been just a couple of blocks away when the towers fell. After the cloud had passed and the plume of pulverized ash had settled, he had organized a makeshift triage station with a small ragtag band of rogue businessmen, cabbies, bus drivers, and folks from the street. The wounded had come soon after, and he had been ready. He'd made sure bandages were prepared and litters were made. Medicines had been gathered for a variety of woes. Whatever came at them, Dr. Mahoney had known his crew could meet it.

"It's okay, people! I'm a doctor! I'm a medical doctor. Now, listen up, people!" he'd raised his voice in authority.

As he had organized his impromptu aid station, he had thought this would have been his finest hour, helping others in a real-time combat situation. Patiently, he and his band of street heroes had waited for the walking wounded. They had waited for the exodus up the avenue; they had been ready to help, bandage, and treat, but nobody had come.

When all was said and done and all of the numbers came in, there had been thousands injured emotionally, scarred by the trauma of what had happened, what they had seen, and what they had lived through. But there had been only a limited number of physically wounded. On that day in a disaster of that magnitude, you either had lived or died. And Dr. Mahoney, despite medical skills, knowledge, and experience, could have done nothing. He had waited and attempted to stave off the weight of the passing time for as long as he could. And then, like so many of us, he had caved in, overwhelmed by immeasurable grief.

And then Annie; a colleague, a nurse, and the wife of an injured man; had called. Now, through his dedicated colleague, he would finally treat a wounded survivor of 9/11. He would be able to counsel a seriously injured firefighter from the firehouse closest to the catastrophe. Quietly, by himself that night, he swore to his God that he would use all his skill and expertise for this one man, the only survivor he could treat. He even celebrated with a bit of fine Irish whiskey as, with tears in his eyes, he finally saw the finish line.

But first, he had to look his patient in the eye.

*   *   *

"Annie, George. Good to see you both again, safe and sound." His voice revealed nothing of his trials, sounding instead strong and authoritative. "George, the Veteran's Administration and the fire department's medical division are treating your other injuries. You're receiving epidural shots for your back, and I see that you'll need a spinal fusion procedure down the line."

He was reading from the official report, information Annie and I knew well.

"The swelling around your head and eye have decreased considerably," he said with certainty, but I felt compelled to respond.

"Yeah, Doc. They took an X-ray of the inside of my head—but they didn't find anything."

I guess I was trying to bring a little levity into the room. My wife looked at me sternly. I straightened up.

"Sorry, Doc. What I mean is, I've received a CAT scan of my head and a myelogram of my spine."

My tone, I hoped, expressed my sorrow, and he nodded, turning now to Annie.

"Annie, how are your husband's sleeping habits these days?"

As a longtime nurse, she pulled no punches.

"His sleep is totally disturbed with bouts of violent nightmares so bad that he has to sleep in another room sometimes. Not to mention he hasn't been able to remember a damn thing about that day." Her tone was disgusted. "But maybe that's for the best, Dr. Mahoney."

"There lies our problem." The doctor looked up. "That's what we have to work on."

Did he know how this one secret would unlock the pain in me and in him? But there was more, and he continued, "I've found out through my sources that if George can't account for himself, he won't be able to testify at the 9/11 Commission, which means he won't be able to be seen by the 9/11 Compensation Board."

A silence fell over Annie and me. We looked at each other, acknowledging in our silence how far we had yet to go.

The doctor continued to speak, "Unfortunately, this might also affect your disability with the fire department as well. I've seen it happen more than once."

As the good doctor shared this, my stomach churned. It was all too much.

"I don't know how we can sit here, Doc," I broke in. "I don't see how we can sit here and talk about *disability* when there are still dead who have not been recovered."

"I can assure you, George," continued Dr. Mahoney in his calm, straightforward manner. "Everything is being done to recover the bodies. Identifying them, of course, is another story. Let me say this, your concern should be for number one right now because if you don't take care of number one, you can't take care of numbers two and three—those, of course, being your lovely wife and the adorable child you have.

"Luckily, right now, there's a logjam of firefighters trying to exit the job. That buys us some time," the doctor continued in a logical and calm manner, "but when the 9/11 Commission asks you to stand in the batter's box and testify under oath, you'd better be able to recall what happened—or you'll lose out."

"What do you suggest, Doctor?" asked Annie, ever practical, with a quiver in her voice.

"There are alternative methodologies for recouping one's memory. I'd like to start you with sleep therapy immediately and then maybe hypnotherapy down the road. And if that doesn't work …" His words slowed a bit. "Have you ever been entranced before, George?"

The good doctor was expecting an answer.

I wasn't sure what he was asking, and so I stalled a bit before responding.

"To answer that honestly, Doctor," I finally replied, "only when I look into my wife's and daughter's eyes."

Annie put her hand in mine, and we all smiled. I'd hit a home run.

"George, we'll start you off with sleep therapy then." Dr. Mahoney's voice sounded kind now as he gave his orders. "I'll just fill out this prescription for a strong sleep aid. Give it to the pharmacist." He wrote, looking down, and kept on talking. "Now, let me just say this before I let you both go: This is sleep *therapy*, so lengthy sleep is key. But that's just the first part. You will also have to confront your dreams, which is not going to be an easy task, not with all you've been through as a survivor and all. And you must keep a journal and write down all your dreams as soon as you've woken up, and that way we can analyze them later.

"You'll be assigned a 9/11 grief counselor." He looked up just in time to see me cringing. "And this is strong medication, so to avoid any depression it may cause, you should take it only once every three or four days or maybe once a week. I've given you a large bottle, so you'll have plenty."

He'd finally finished with me and turned toward my wife.

"Annie, please call. Stay in touch. I want to know immediately if there's any change in recall."

He thanked us both for coming in as we thanked him. We stood, I shook his hand, and we left the office. Something had fused us together, I realized while leaving the building. Doctor, nurse, and patient were now 9/11 brothers and sisters.

*　　　*　　　*

CHAPTER 3
Continue Firing Your Weapon!

I missed a lot of funerals before I was able to move around well. I missed the funerals of guys I had fought fires with, guys whose children's christenings I had attended, guys I had laughed and cried with in the late 1970s, 1980s, and 1990s. They were family men and the greatest firefighters and officers you'd ever meet.

After all was said and done, there were almost two years of solid funerals, as well as memorials and Masses that are still celebrated annually. As soon as I could move about, I tried to go to as many as I could. First, I went to the memorial Mass for Chief Casper, who was a family friend, with my wife and daughter. Then I made the mistake of trying to attend the funeral of Ladder 10's Shawn Tallon, who had been a probationary firefighter at Ten House and years before had already proven himself as a Marine. He was a hero to me and to many others, and he was one of the members of Ten House who had fallen that day. But I was pushing myself too hard, too fast. When the pain from my head, back, and neck became overwhelming, I had to excuse myself from the funeral formation. I came home limping with tears in my eyes and beer on my breath.

"This is too much for you right now," she scolded.

"I'm sorry, baby. I wanted to say good-bye to the proby." As if by way of apology I added, "I thought it would help me remember."

When the day of Captain Patty Brown's funeral came, I knew I had to try again. Captain Patrick Brown had been a fellow Vietnam vet and a friend to Annie and me. I'd had the honor of working with Patty in the early 1990s when he had toured Brooklyn and he was a young fire lieutenant. In view of our history, Annie bit her lip and, with a look of reservation, gave me the okay to attend. She knew it wouldn't be easy for me, physically or mentally, and she didn't want me to mess myself up further by drowning my sorrow in alcohol. She phrased it in military terms: I had a mission that day. My mission was to bring home a Mass card from Patty Brown's funeral, and I had to make it home and pass on the beer.

I okayed the hell out of her, accepted the terms, and promised to be on my best behavior before heading over to Manhattan. Patty's funeral was nothing less than majestic. It seemed the entire New York City Fire Department had turned out for the rescue captain, a man who many feel topped its all-time hero list.

To start with, there was the setting: St. Patrick's Cathedral, New York, New York. Its soaring stone steeples; intricate carvings; and huge, ornate stained glass windows face Manhattan's already pretty grand Fifth Avenue like a visitation from another century. Even those without a trace of religion felt awe when they looked up at its spires and the arches that reached for something higher. And on that day, the stone cathedral was not simply alone, greeting my fellow firefighters and me. No, it was surrounded, supported, and brought to life by a turnout the size of which did the Department honor.

Several division-size formations composed of service men and women of all imaginable stripes were posted on Fifth Avenue, leading up to the Cathedral. There, out front, I saw the uniforms of members from all branches of the Armed Forces with their color guards holding their flags proudly. Firefighters and representatives from other states joined them. Naturally, the New York City Police Department showed up to honor him, as did a contingent of New York State Troopers. Representatives from the fire brigades of England, Germany, Ireland, and Holland were there to show respect as well. Many of these service people flanked the great stone cathedral, spilling out onto the sidewalk in front and letting all who passed on Fifth Avenue know that a man of merit was being honored. Inside, the cathedral was crammed full with even more dignitaries, politicians, religious figures, and members of our department: all there for Patty Brown.

In department lore, his name had already taken on mythic proportions. It was part of the fire department vernacular. When a firefighter executes a certain roof rope rescue technique, for example, he or she is now "pulling a Patty Brown." In fact, such is the pure love and admiration with which the man is remembered, that any act of courage is now "a Patty Brown."

That day, standing beside my fellow firefighters, something inside me started ringing like an alarm clock. In retrospect, it was probably my captive memory, struggling to free itself from the barriers my healing body and mind had erected in its way. My head ached; the ringing in it was nearly unbearable. But because of my pride, I was holding myself together externally. I looked pretty nifty in my firefighter's Class A uniform with my Vietnam citations, my Purple Heart, Combat Infantryman Badge, Airborne Wings, and unit patch on my lapel. Despite my injuries, three honorable mentions, and more than twenty-seven years on the job, I had no named firefighting medals. I'd come close more than a couple of times. "Always a bridesmaid, never a bride," I used to say. But I had my Class A, my Class B's, and my unit citations. Those might be considered low level, but I considered them a holy configuration with the big Ten House patch rounding it out. (That patch has its own story: Designed before 9/11, it shows a redheaded firefighter standing astride the Twin Towers with one leg on the North Tower and the other on the South. The firefighter is the symbol of Ten House, and this patch is the most sought-after unit patch on the job.) That day, the Ten House patch commanded more respect than many other honors. High-ranking officers spotted it and saluted me. They understood what it meant.

After a couple of times, I wondered if it meant something more. I started to salute back and then approach them.

"Hey, Chief, about my overtime ..." I began. "I could use a night tour."

Invariably, they brushed off my banter and asked, "Were you there that day?"

"Yes," I responded, "but I can't remember."

"Who are you shittin', pal? You just don't wanna remember!"

At the time, that made more sense than the reality I knew to be the truth. But reality is an odd thing, and that day in that holy place while we gathered to pay respect to a man we all loved, I realized the truth of it. It then hit me that no matter where I go, I will always be known as the surviving firefighter from the house closest to Ground Zero. In an effort to regroup, I repeated what has become my personal mantra, "I'm glad to be here. In fact, I'm glad to be anywhere."

And I was glad to be there. Particularly as the Honorable Mayor Rudolph Giuliani took the podium on the altar and addressed the massive crowd. I stood outside with hundreds of other uniforms, huddled close and clamoring to hear and see what was going on. But even outside on the steps and side halls of the gigantic cathedral, we were able to participate. Some organizer with forethought had set up speakers on the stone steps of the cathedral, and we listened as each voice came out of them, crackling with the distance and electricity. We surrounded St. Patrick's, and when the final prayer started, each man and woman in uniform bowed his or her head and placed their white-gloved hands in solidarity on the backs of those who stood to their left and to their right. Those white gloves made visible the ocean of brotherhood surrounding St. Patrick's that day, a human wave that crested and broke on the altar.

I was part of that brotherhood, I felt that prayer, and I bowed my head with my colleagues. But for a moment, when I closed my eyes, I was no longer on the steps of that great cathedral. I trembled briefly and was transported. I left the stone steps and found myself once again in a steaming jungle. I was back in Vietnam. It could've been Tay Ninh. It could have been Khe Sanh, Pleiku, or even somewhere along the Ho Chi Minh Trail. Shit, it could have been Cambodia.

All I knew was that I was in position, kneeling behind a large tree that had been downed by artillery ordinance. I was clutching my M16 close to my chest and could smell sulfur from the fierce firefight that was in progress. I remembered a passage from the Special Forces Survival Handbook. It quoted the grandfather of unconventional warfare, Che Guevara, the Cuban revolutionary, "Once inside the hideous firefight, you must fight as if you are already dead and fighting just to become alive again."

Sergeant Patty Brown, dressed in tiger fatigues, stood behind a jungle tree about twenty feet from me, firing his M16 with unbridled passion.

"Hey, Sarge! Hey, *Sarge! Sergeant Brown!"* I screamed.

The Irishman secured his weapon and then turned to look at me. His chiseled face and piercing eyes found me.

"Sarge, throw me a magazine, would ya?"

"Where's your ammo, troop?" He yelled back. "Where's your rucksack? Wait, don't tell me. Back at the base, isn't it, fuckup?"

Just then a hail of AK-47 rounds hit the tree directly in front of Patty. He threw me a bandolier with a full complement of magazines. I was locked and loaded. As suddenly as it happened, an RPG round from Charlie's B40 bazooka suddenly slammed into my tree, exploding like the Fourth of July. We returned fire. We got off a couple of rounds, but from our positions as we were trying to draw a bead on the enemy, we saw a whole regiment of North Vietnamese Army (NVA) foot soldiers in the open field running toward us.

"What do you wanna do, Sarge?" I was screaming at the top of my lungs.

He was yelling an order, but I was still deaf from the RPG explosion. As my hearing returned, I heard Sergeant Brown's voice. It was getting louder and louder as he kept firing.

"Continue firing your weapon! *Continue firing your weapon, damn it!*"

*   *   *

It was dusk when I rang the doorbell to our Brooklyn home. There was a fresh breeze blowing down from the park. Annie came to the door and let me in.

"How do you feel, Daddy?" she asked, scanning my face for clues.

"I'm okay, Mommy."

"Did you complete your mission?"

"I have a thumping headache, Irish," I admitted. I turned to look for her in the darkness of the foyer. "It was hard, mighty hard. But I had a dry event in case you wanted to know, Irish."

I put my arms around her. I knew my kiss confirmed the absence of alcohol on my breath.

"Don't lose any of your ribbons, Daddy," she whispered in my chest. "The baby's sleeping. Don't wake her up. And where's my funeral card?"

Her voice was kind, and from the inside pocket of my uniform, I pulled out the Mass card with the picture of Patty, who was grinning from ear to ear, and handed it to Annie.

"You're not gonna cry, are you?" I said as gently as possible.

"Not now," she replied, looking down at the card. "Maybe later."

We climbed the carpeted stairs to our second-floor kitchen. Annie fixed me something to eat, hung up my uniform, and then escorted me upstairs. Together, we checked on Tara, who was sound asleep.

I turned to Annie and whispered, "She's big for her age. She'll be talking in phrases before we know it."

Annie and I have been Park Slope residents all our lives. Our station in life has been that of civil servants. We have taken pledges to our profession that we believe in, as hokey as that may sound. We have embraced diversity and watched as the neighborhood changed and then changed again. Now, we were a family that needed to heal from the worst attack on American soil since Pearl Harbor. Like many others we knew, it was time to pull together. Staring down at Tara, we knew it was time, this time, to "Pull a Patty Brown."

CHAPTER 4
A Family Beatles Dance Party

Annie had been briefed as well as could be expected. Among her family and friends and the pool of professional colleagues she had accrued during her more than twenty years on the job, she had a formidable resource base to draw on. Throw in her own work experience in No. 9 Metro Tech's medical division of the New York City Fire Department headquarters, and she had a veritable army of nurses and doctors with hundreds of years' worth of experience to collectively draw on.

To them, she once asked a simple question: What could she do with me? What did a wife, a nurse, a loving spouse do with a wounded and scarred husband, a dedicated firefighter, whose injuries went deeper than the bandages and braces; who was deeply depressed and haunted; and whose memory had still not caught up with the trauma that his body, and his city, had suffered?

Physical therapy definitely was on the horizon. There would be psychological counseling as well to deal with the unfathomable experience and overwhelming loss. But these were not immediate solutions. It would take years, and I think Annie was looking for something to start now and begin to bring her husband back.

Annie was no coward and never had been. She wanted to face our problems head on. She had still been on maternity leave with Tara on September 11. And now, with me wounded, her leave had been extended. She had had time to care for us both. But what should she do? I found out later that Kathy, one of her closest nursing friends, suggested a simple approach.

"For Christ's sake, Annie, the whole country is wounded!" she told Annie over the phone while shuffling papers at work. "Count your blessings, honey. Have a good time. Have a party. A fiesta!"

Annie then let the idea roll around in her head. *We do have a lot to be thankful for. George is alive; he is home. But a party? Now, when I have him to care for—on top of all my regular maternal cares for baby Tara? We clearly aren't in a party frame of mind. No ...*

*   *   *

Annie, like so many of us, hadn't yet taken in all that had happened. Who among us could conceive right then of the enormity of the attack—that thousands of people had been killed and that hundreds of firefighters were still unaccounted for. The reality was still too big for any of us to truly wrap our minds around. But Annie was not and never has been naïve.

After I had left for work that morning and reported for a day tour at Ladder Ten, she'd turned the television on in time to see the second plane hit the South Tower. She'd felt that flash of bewilderment and rage that our entire country felt, and for her it had turned immediately into a frozen fear. "George's Ten House," as she always had called it, stood on the corner of Liberty Street, right across the street from the South Tower. *What will happen to George's firehouse, a relatively small, brick oasis of safety, in the shadow of that towering and wounded steel and glass giant?*

In retrospect if asked, she remembers how calm she was. She remembers that she prayed, sharing a little private time with Jesus while she sat holding our curly-haired little girl. Within minutes, her sister called, trying to offer comfort in the confusion of the day. She remembers little of what was actually said.

"Try not to worry too much," she recalls her sister saying, "not until you get the word."

She had put baby Tara down by the time she saw the towers collapse to the ground in their unnatural columns of thunder and dust. We are both grateful that the baby was safely in bed as she faced the horror. *All is lost,* she thought for a moment as the horrendous image replayed on the television and in her mind's eye. *All is lost.*

She made herself turn away and look down at Tara with her round face still innocent of the world and at peace. Tara was our miracle baby, born after years of trying to conceive and spent on an emotional rollercoaster as we navigated the ups and downs of contemporary fertility sciences. Tara brought her back to earth to the here and now. As she did for us both in the days to come, Tara helped her regain control and kept her grounded and sane at that moment of crisis. (Later, she found additional comfort in the fact that I had come home when so many others hadn't. I was alive even as so many we knew were not. And I would be well again someday even if the path toward that healing was a long one.)

*   *   *

Yes, I was home and I would heal. But I was depressed and despondent, and the huge gaping holes in my memory had begun their torment. So while we were waiting for the healing and the therapy to begin and for the days and years to come forth, what could we do to put our lives back together? Of all her friends, family, and contacts, nobody had had a better idea. So maybe, just maybe, a family party was the way to kick off our new post-9/11 life. It was more than a celebration. It was an exorcism and proof positive that love, family life, and simple humanity were enough to drive the darkness away. Maybe it was even enough to drive the devil out of our hearts and away from our shores—at least for one night.

And so, somewhere in the back of Annie's ever-practical mind, the questions began to distill, not just "Should we have a party?" but "How would we put such a 'do' together?" Annie was Annie, the super-competent nurse, wife, and mother, and once the logistics were formulated, the deal was inevitably sealed.

How would I plan such a party? she asked herself, beginning to accept that the idea had taken root. *Maybe it could be just an informal get-together, maybe candles or balloons ...*

After dinner on a Thursday, Annie excused herself from the table without telling me why.

"Would you mind feeding Tara?" she asked.

"It would be my pleasure, Mommy," I replied already in a better mood.

Handing our jolly baby over, she headed off downstairs. Our basement is, well, a basement, and Annie isn't too fond of the water bugs and other creatures that sometimes lurk in the dark. But when she set herself to task, she's as courageous as any, and that night she braved its depths, poking about fearlessly and turning a deaf ear to any odd scurry or scuffle. In the back of the cellar she found what she was looking for: a large box marked "Candles" from which she chose eight, including two scented ones. She also found a neatly rolled throw rug. A quick peek at its decorative center revealed it was a long-ago souvenir of the Kennedy administration. The rug showed John F. Kennedy in the Oval Office next to a large presidential seal. Perfect!

Once she'd brought them upstairs, she rolled out the rug, making an impromptu presidential dance floor in our parlor and rolled in what looked like a huge, old-fashioned Victrola, but which in reality is our CD player. The scene was set.

"Mommy! Tara ate all her foodsy!"

I was a bit giddy by the time Annie came back to the kitchen. Not that I didn't take all my fathering duties seriously, but I'd begun to wonder where my wife had gone.

"Okay, Daddy!" Annie greeted us both with a big smile but without revealing her secrets. "After you wipe the baby's mouth and you both digest a little, you can come upstairs to the parlor for a surprise."

One look at Annie's face told me that she'd got something planned. She was aglow and hardly able to contain her glee. I turned our baby around on my lap and looked at those sparkling eyes.

"See, I told you, Tara." The baby was smiling at me, but she wasn't saying anything either. "I told you there was going to be a big dance party tonight."

"Now, how did you guess that?" Annie asked with dismay.

"Tara and I heard you rolling in the big Victrola," I explained as I pointed to the ceiling above. "What do you think you're dealing with here? A bunch of amateurs?"

In my giddiness, I slipped into serious Brooklynese; my "what do you" came out more like a nasal honk, "whaddaya think?" But Annie's smile had returned, and little Tara was beaming with delight at all of the attention, too.

Now, neither Tara, nor I were able to make with any speed that night, me with my injuries, and her still needing to be carried. So it took a while before we were all upstairs. Once in the parlor though, it only took a moment to decide what would play. The carousel spun around and stopped at our favorite homemade Beatles song collection. They were in no specific order. *Sergeant Pepper* was mixed with early Beatles; *White Album* was mixed with rarities and *Rubber Soul.*

A steady hard drum beat started leading to the song "Birthday" from *the White Album.* And as the guitar riff began baby Tara began to bounce up and down in a Babies Gone Wild dancing motion. A minute or two down the line father and daughter were imitating Chubby Checkers' twisting motion to The Beatles' early rendition of "Twist and Shout."

We, banged-up Daddy and baby Tara, were twisting on the presidential seal, as our dance party got under way.

Annie entered the parlor as the candlelight flickered; the slight breeze of her movement made diamonds of the soft light with the chandelier overhead. My voice echoed through our huge, old parlor, adding another element to the light, the music, and the bizarre carpet underfoot. We were in our own world, slapdash maybe, but echoing with love. And then I noticed what had been keeping Annie. She was carrying a tray. On it was a bowl of ice cubes, two tall glasses, a bottle of carbonated soda, and another of Baileys Irish Cream liqueur. *This truly is a rare occasion,* I thought to myself.

Twisting baby Tara over to her mom, I yelled above the music, "Hey, Mommy! Are we gonna make milkshakes?"

She smiled and laughed and, sure enough, began her mixing magic. A couple of minutes later, Annie and I were sipping on our grown-up shakes while Tara enjoyed the rug, doing what we've dubbed the "booty dance" while Ringo Starr sang "We all live in a yellow submarine."

Annie ran off to find Tara's angel wings, the soft feathery appendages that so match the beautific glow on her little face. They were in the toy room, and Annie found a disposable flash camera there, too. Tara was

still getting down—she had her parents' appreciation of the classics—
and Annie got some quick photos in.

She was rocking to the beat, still maybe a bit unsteady on her feet.
Swaying back and forth, as The Beatles sang "Get Back," their roof top
hit from 1969.

How could we resist? Giggling at the sight of Tara's dance, we put
down our drinks to join her on our knees.. We celebrated by joining
hands. "Ring Around the Rosie" works just as well with the rhythm,
and the Bailey's didn't hurt Daddy either. Finally, "Penny Lane" came
on, the only Beatles song that mentions firemen and nurses. The energy
we dispensed was calling us to end our little dance party. I couldn't help
reflect on the line "And the fireman rushing in from the pouring rain,
very strange." We gathered up our things, shut the lights and music,
and started our bedtime routine.

The magic of family can make a man forget all the evil in the world
and can make him dismiss even for one night all the hatred. Singing
and dancing with my family, I could feel the spirits of all of the good
people we have known and all of their kindness. In Tara's face, I saw
them all—memories like joyful children, longing to dance free.

She's a stunner, I thought of our little Tara. *It's no wonder really that
she can take me away.* Over time, we had grown used to the regular
comments from passers-by. "You've got a Shirley Temple look-alike!"
they'd say as they admired her bouncing banana curls and twinkling
eyes for the first time. "Yeah," we'd say. We were so used to it. It's her
round cheeks, dimpling up as she smiles, and the way her cherry lips
open when she laughs. She was our little starlet and a born entertainer,
made for center stage.

Of course, Annie and I relate to her more as "Little Miss Late for
Dinner," and that has nothing to do with how well she eats. I was

approaching my fifties before she came along, and Annie and I had been trying to start a family for years. As anyone else who has faced similar hurdles will know, once you're committed, trying to have a baby can seem to go from the world's most natural act to its most expensive sport. And in addition to all of the expense, the doctors' appointments and the discomfort can put potential parents in the center of a tug of war between Mother Nature and Father Science. We were on an emotional rollercoaster, and somewhere between the highs of hope and the lows of disappointment we'd almost given up. I started drinking in response; it was all too much. But finally, all our work and vigilance, not to mention all of science's advances, paid off. Tara Bridget Bachmann was born during the summer, barely two months before 9/11. Looking back, she is so much more a miracle now. Did she, our little darling, know how much I would need a smile like hers? How those dimpled cheeks would be like a lifeline to me after all the horror and the loss?

I was pretty beat up—no doubt about it—and had miles more to go before I'd even be halfway the man I'd once been. But that night as I watched my little star dance, I knew that all was right for me in this world. No matter what nightmares loomed, I had Annie and now my baby to dance away the pain.

CHAPTER 5

The 9/11 Grief Counselor

The following morning we were back to reality and fast. Dr. Mahoney called, asking Annie if my condition had changed at all and if my sleep was still erratic. Despite our marvelous night, she had to report that my sleep was still broken. I wasn't getting better. It's time for the next step, the doctor ordered, and he gave Annie the contact information for a grief counselor.

A few days later, I had my first appointment. Neither the setting, nor the counselor was what I expected. The Upper East Side clinic on East 64th Street was a different world from Brooklyn and certainly more than a few subway stops from Ground Zero. Susan Miller, my counselor, didn't look like Dr. Mahoney. Tall and pretty with short blond hair and long, lovely legs, she was a licensed social worker, and she started right in. Although Dr. Mahoney had briefed her about my history and about his ideas of sleep therapy, she needed to assess the patient for herself.

"George."

So we are going to be on a first-name basis? I thought of her as "Mrs. Miller."

"Dr. Mahoney told me about your recall, about your light amnesia."

So he called it "light"? That was news to me. The assessment was correct insomuch as I had short-term memory loss. I was able to remember the rest of my life, but I just couldn't make myself remember that one awful day.

"Forgive me for saying so," she continued, "but the dark circles around your eyes indicate to me that you haven't been sleeping well."

I could tell she was trying to be gentle.

"It's been tough, but they tell me I should be grateful."

How could I be anything but brave in front of someone like her? But this lovely lady was a grief counselor. Although she had not had any actual direct experience with 9/11 on-site survivors, she did have extensive experience working with many of the bereaved families.

"Well, where should we start?" she asked.

I smiled at her but kept my mouth shut.

"Maybe you could give me a brief history of yourself, George?"

She was trying to see if I was in the mood to open up. I wasn't, particularly.

"Just a short verbal outline will do."

She wasn't taking silence for an answer. I considered for a moment how angry Annie would be if this didn't work, especially if it didn't work because I hadn't even tried! Maybe it was the caffeine or knowing how much my dear wife wanted me to get better, get my memory back, and heal. Maybe it was, just a little bit, my desire to impress the pretty lady. At any rate, I started to talk.

"Well, Mrs. Miller—"

"Please, call me Susan."

Now that I was going to talk, she acted sweet as meringue pie.

"Well, Susan," I began with the slow, stalling manner my wife would have recognized immediately. Maybe Mrs. Miller—Susan—did, too, but she gave me the time I needed. I spent a moment taking in my surroundings. *Did Annie know that she'd sent me to see such a fine figure of a woman? Better not go there.*

Before I started, she interrupted quickly, saying, "You're not related to the Bachman Turner Overdrive, the famous 1970s rock group, are you?"

I laughed at the familiar quip and replied, "No, I'm not, but you could say I am 'taking care of business.'" After that, I dived in. "I had a good childhood. There was no abuse or anything like that. But my stepfather—a Navy man—was stern." I gave her the brief rundown on my father, a marine. "He was killed in action in Korea when I was merely a toddler, not long after the birth of my brother, Johnny. My mother remarried, and they had another boy and a girl, my stepbrother and stepsister. My stepfather, although a good man, could be both cold and demanding." I paused for a breath. "I could have used more love, but I guess we could all have used more love from our parents, right?"

I was trying to sound mature. I had my own family now; I was a father, too. I understood the pressures.

"Okay, I'm rambling. I'll try to stick to the point. I came not from a rich family, but we had plenty."

I told her then about growing up in Brooklyn but also how we escaped the city in the summer, camping out on the beaches of Montauk. There, on the tip of Long Island, we fished for blowfish, blues, and flatfish, surfcasting in the waves. I recalled participating in casting tournaments, standing in the wet sand with my fishing rods, and casting for the riches of the Atlantic. When I was eleven, a friend of my family, the famous white shark hunter and record holder Frank

Mundus, extracted a fishing hook from my thumb and gave me a gentle slap on the back of the head for crying about it. I was officially a fisherman. I did some hunting during those summers, too, off in the woods behind those beaches. I don't recall ever hitting anything; I was only armed with a BB gun. I always felt that my forays into the forest had put me in touch with Mother Nature. In Vietnam, I had reason to be grateful for this familiarity—unlike some of my colleagues, being alone in the jungle never bothered me.

It wasn't all idyllic. I became a paratrooper partly to get back at my Marine father, who had never returned from Korea. The marines and the paratroopers were known to fight like cats and dogs. I found this to be true when I became a paratrooper at Fort Bragg in Fayetteville, North Carolina. My stepsister had become a homicide statistic in Brooklyn while I was in the Army after my tour in Vietnam. That effectively ended my military career; I needed to care for my mother.

Letters home from Vietnam

Dear Mom,

I know you're still mad at me for dropping out of high school, but good news! Tonight is prom night on the Ho Chi Minh Trail. Bad news: this guy is the chaperone. First Sargent says, "Everyone must dance!"

Love, Bucksargent Georgie Bachmann / Age 19

But it was all part and parcel of growing up. I told her about my teenage band made up of a group of buddies and how we did our best, banging out our versions of The Beatles and the Stones for fun and to impress the neighborhood's young ladies. Then I told her about dropping out of high school and not being able to wait until I could join the army and go to Vietnam. I told her about being medevacked home to Walter Reed Army Medical Center at the end of my tour with shrapnel in my leg from a B40 bazooka and in my back from a mortar attack. I went back but was finally sent home with dual malaria. I told her about my scars and about my second Purple Heart, following the mortar attack.

"I bummed around at a few civilian jobs in the 1970s," I continued. "Then I decided to become a New York City firefighter. I was never one of those kids who prayed for a fire truck under the Christmas tree, but my Vietnam experience shaped me. I had seen people on fire; I had wanted to help them. The idea began to take hold, but I may never have moved forward if it hadn't been for George Williams of Squad One, a Vietnam vet himself who served with the Big Red One. A proud African American, he dragged me down to Worth St. on the last day to register for the New York City Firefighter exam. George was also the best man at our wedding." I went on, telling Mrs. Miller all about the application process and about taking the test with 20,000 other people and coming in at number 219. "Mayor Abe Beam was in office then, and everything had slowed down. The city was laying off, not hiring civil servants. It was a two-year wait before I finally got in. It was 1976. Six weeks of training followed, which largely focused on the physical skills needed although there was some book study required. We learned to slide off of roofs and rappel down ropes and how to use the tools and apparatus of the trade. I was on the job.

Firefighter George Bachmann Waiting on a signal 1999

"I stayed with the same Brooklyn firehouse from the 1970s on through the 1990s." I told her how the firehouse and borough felt like home. "There was plenty of fire duty there, too. We were in the top twenty-five busiest firehouses in the city for three decades. We often broke through to the top ten.

"Then, in 1991, I married an Irish chatterbox, Annie. She's one of the senior nurses in the department—"

Mrs. Miller stopped me then and asked me to continue our discussion of my work before I deviated into my marriage.

"If you don't mind me asking, George, how did you end up at Ladder 10 in Lower Manhattan?"

I sighed. Here was one of the points I'd been hoping to gloss over. But, well, it was all connected.

"Well, Mrs. Miller," I began—she was just going to have to accept that in some ways I'm an old-fashioned guy—"I guess it sort of spiraled out of control. I mean it wasn't a nightmare of biblical proportions, but things got pretty bad.

"I had never been in any kind of criminal trouble in my life." I felt she had to understand where I was coming from. "*Never*. And looking back now, I guess if I were looking for an excuse, I could say it was stress. I mean I can see what I did; I can see the error of my ways, but basically, I was blindsided by all of the stress when Annie and I were trying to have our baby. We kept on failing. Nothing was working. *Nothing*—and yet all the 'experts,'" I couldn't help putting a little spin on that word, "kept saying that there shouldn't be a problem. But there was; something wasn't working. And it was taking a toll on both of us." I had to be honest. "Well, on me in particular.

"They came for me and arrested me in my Brooklyn firehouse in late May 2000, it was the same night as the Wendy's massacre in Queens. The Wendy's massacre was the lead story that night and unfortunately, I was the second lead story. I was accused of using and selling drugs, which was preposterous." There, I'd gotten the worst part of it out. "It was insane," I told her. "They couldn't find any drugs in the firehouse or in my residence. What hurt their case even more is that there weren't any drugs in my system."

Her questioning look said it all, *So if there were no drugs, why you?*

"I believe I was selected, hand-picked if you will, out of a small group of recreational users because they wanted to make an example out of someone."

She raised an eyebrow, but it made sense.

"I was the only one in the group who didn't have any family on the job. Unlike some others, my father wasn't a captain or a chief. My brother wasn't a lieutenant.

"And, hey, I'd been having some problems. I was drinking a bit too much, as I've already told you. But I think the crux is this: At the time, I'd been serving with a particularly aggressive young lieutenant. He had a reputation as a hardass if you'll excuse my language."

Mrs. Miller nodded, silently urging me to continue.

"He was the kind of officer who would have inspections every morning before nine o'clock roll call just to check and see if you were wearing the right color socks. Everything had to be by the book.

"Later, I heard that he was swearing a blue streak attesting to my innocence. He had this heavy *Sopranos*-style accent, 'You fuckin' mean to tell me that my senior man, a guy who never goes sick and does a better than average job at a fire is a fuckin' drug kingpin? No! Horse shit!'

"But even having my hardass lieutenant's belief in me didn't stop it and didn't stop them from leaking it to the media. And they jumped on the story: a New York City firefighter selling drugs right out of the firehouse to other firefighters and to civilians? Sheesh."

I couldn't help shuddering as I remembered all of the hoopla. My friends and our families saw it on television. They read it in the papers.

"Please go on, George." Mrs. Miller was busy taking notes, but at least she didn't appear to be phased by the whole thing.

"I was counseled by my fire department lawyer to settle. He swore that if I went along with the whole program, he could have me back in the firehouse and back on the job in just a couple of months. So I did it."

She didn't look up, just kept writing her notes.

"First, I had to sign a paper saying that I was found to have illicit substances in my possession even though there were no drugs to be found and no drugs in me when they tested me. Then I went through the system. I did a short stint with a five-star, top-of-the-line rehab, went to some AA meetings, and did a little community service just to prove I was worthy of the status of a peace officer, which is a firefighter's position in the community. It was all crap, but I don't know maybe I learned a little something about managing stress. Sometimes when you lay down with the dogs, you catch fleas.

"At any rate, once things calmed down, Annie and I did two more in vitro fertilizations, and both procedures failed. Then on the third try, when our finances were nearly rock bottom and our emotions shredded, something happened. My Annie was suddenly, miraculously with child.

"What with everything that had been going on and now with everything that was starting to happen, it didn't seem like there was any time to celebrate. There were cribs to be put together and rooms to be painted. I was finishing up the last of my community service, and soon I was to be reinstated and sworn in once again at the fire department headquarters. I was scheduled for counseling with Father Mychal Judge in the Fire Department's counseling unit.

"I began the necessary retraining course on the 'Rock,' or Randall's Island, out in the harbor. And then I was assigned to a firehouse. It was the summer of 2001. By chance, my assignment came through for a firehouse in Lower Manhattan—Ten House. My first tour back as a firefighter was a night tour. After my gear was stowed away in my locker, I was given a position on the rig, and then the officers and all of the senior men briefed me.

"I still remember that night. It was around ten thirty by the time everything had settled in. I'd already called to check in with my very pregnant wife, and I'd decided to go to the front door for a last breath of the night air before going up to the bunk room. I had my hands in my pocket, and I was reveling in the turn of events. I thought about how good it felt to be back in uniform! Annie's pregnancy was going smoothly. I was wondering what the baby would be like, and how our life would change with this addition to our family. With these thoughts in mind, I looked up as if to thank heaven for my blessings. As I took another deep breath my eyes fell on the huge, hulking megastructure across the street that was hiding another giant megastructure behind it. The two of them were both so large that they dwarfed my firehouse and me. They were that close: The South Tower is a stone's throw from the corner of Liberty, where I stood in front of Ten House. We were so small in comparison, and I stood there looking up, awed by its immensity. The world and I had broken even. All was good, despite the difficult ride, and my faith was restored in God and in man."

I stopped talking then and looked over at Mrs. Miller.

"To tell you the truth, Susan," I said, giving it a try. "That's one of my last memories. Annie's delivery went well. There were no complications. She gave birth at Methodist Hospital, where she worked as an emergency room nurse on a per diem status, and I was there to help. I know that we were all healthy and happy. The very last thing I remember was not long after the birth of our little Tara. Sometime later that same summer, we, Annie, Tara, and me, were having our picture taken on the steps of our home. My wife has since told me that this was on Tara's christening day."

I fell silent and watched her note-taking catch up. She scribbled; I watched. Finally, she looked up and, for just a moment, looked at me in silence. Then she switched gears.

"Now, George," she said, "I'm interested in how you feel now about fate."

She maintained her professional calm, but there was a poignancy and a sense of effort to her question. But I had given her everything I could recall—my life's story in a session—and I felt drained and aggravated.

"Well, it's been my experience, Susan, that fate can serve you happiness on a silver platter one day and then deliver a swift kick in the chiclets the next."

I was cranky and could hear the sarcasm in my own voice. But she laughed.

"Good, good." She started writing again. "Are you ready to start your sleep therapy this week?"

"I was born ready, Susan."

My energy was returning. Maybe this talk had helped.

"Great." She gave me a smile, and I felt amply rewarded. "I'll tell Dr. Mahoney that you're good to go!"

We stood then and shook hands, and she saw me to the door.

Good to go where? I asked myself as the question nagging at my tired mind. But I only waved good-bye and then limped over to the subway train, back to Brooklyn and back to my waiting family.

CHAPTER 6
The Wizard of Oz in the Lobby and Stairwell

"Annie! Annie!" I cracked the bathroom door a few inches and yelled down. I was on the third floor, and Annie was downstairs, tending to Tara. It was bedtime in the Bachmann household. "We're out of toilet paper up here."

After all, in some ways, we were still a normal family. And right now, I was having the kind of minor crisis that every family goes through.

"Annie! Bring me up some toilet paper!"

"Okay. Okay," she responded from below.

She gathered up a few rolls and started up the stairs. Stuck there, with little else to do, I turned the empty roll into a makeshift kazoo and serenaded my darling wife with an impromptu version of The Beatles' "Honey Pie" while she thumped her way upstairs. Relief was at hand. She bumped the door with her hip, swinging it wide open.

"Hey, I'm doing my business in here, Irish!"

"Do you want your paper or not?"

No nonsense, my wife. She handed me a roll and started stacking the extras in the cabinet. It was a normal night and a normal crisis was resolved. About six weeks had passed since the meeting with the grief counselor, and I still hadn't tried the sleep therapy. *I am stalling, but things are getting back to normal, aren't they? We are doing okay, aren't we?*

But then came the kicker, the wifely ultimatum.

"Listen, before you come to bed, I want you to do something."

"Don't worry. I'll wipe."

I was trying to be funny, but my joke fell flat. It was clear she wasn't in a joking mood. She didn't even pause.

"I want you to take the sleeping medication tonight. I told Dr. Mahoney I'd make you take it."

I counteroffered, "Look, what if I take a big slug of the cherry NyQuil we've got in the medicine cabinet instead?"

She saw the look in my eyes. She knew I didn't want to go there—that deep. But she couldn't let me off this time. The word was out that the 9/11 Commission was calling people down to No. 9 Metro Tech, and my name was on the call list.

"No!" she responded firmly but calmly. She was in her nursing mode—stern and strict. "You have to heal. You have to heal for me and for the baby. If you take the NyQuil, you'll be up at three in the morning, pacing around and drinking coffee." She knew how I was. The restless nights had been going on for several months by that point. "I want you to take one of those big, blue horse pills that the doctor prescribed."

She took the pill bottle out of the medicine cabinet and sat it on the sink.

"And anything else, nurse?" From outside of myself, I could hear the sarcasm in my voice, and it wasn't pleasant. "Can I have some privacy now?"

"Yes," she remained calm, still the professional. "Please spray when you're done in here."

As she made her way downstairs, I completed my rendition of "Honey Pie."

"Thanks for the paper, Irish," I yelled after her. "My hiney was getting itchy!"

Once she was gone, I got ready for bed. I washed my hands and, for some reason, gave myself a quick shave—not my usual pre-bedtime routine. Maybe I was looking to delay whatever was coming.

God, this is hard. I stared at the bottle of NyQuil. *Won't this do the trick? No, I made promises to Annie and to Tara, and it's time to act on them.* Ignoring the triangular dark-red bottle, I reached for the blue pill instead.

"Down the hatch," I said to myself and swallowed.

It took some time to limp downstairs to our bedroom—another reminder of the healing still to be done. Getting around, and certainly up and down stairs, remained a challenge. At the same time, these stairs, this brownstone, and everything around me reminded me that I should be grateful. I had a home and a family, and I was here with them.

In my own time, I made it to the big bedroom where my wife and baby had waited. They greeted me with happy smiles, and Tara, ready to play, jumped on me. Mom stopped her, gently reminding her that she had to be careful of my injuries. The bandages were off, but I was still hobbling pretty badly and working hard at my regular physical therapy.

"You don't want to hurt your daddy's back, do you?"

But some things were not beyond me.

"Family hug time!" I yelled.

I held them both close.

"I took the pill, Annie," I told her with my arms still around them both. "You'll have to put Tara in her crib after she falls asleep. I'm afraid of what I'll be like in a few— I might be flailing my arms or something."

"I'll take care of it." Annie was smiling. "You rest, so you can heal. Where's your journal?"

"Downstairs, Mommy."

She nodded, and I knew she'd get it for me.

"Make some kind of entry in it even if you don't have anything to report." She was looking sleepy herself. "We have to keep Dr. Mahoney happy."

Tara grabbed the TV remote as Mom turned down the light. As a family, we cuddled together, and the DVD started with a familiar tune.

"Oh this!" I laughed with surprise. *Had the pill started in already?*

"I got this down the avenue at Blockbuster." Annie whispered, seeking my approval. "I wanted Tara to see it. It's good kid stuff."

She didn't need to justify her choice to me. I was beaming as the classic film began. Judy Garland, still young and vivacious, in her Kansas home with her adventures about to begin. The 1939 classic was a hit from the start. Tara particularly loved Dorothy's little dog, Toto.

"Doggie Da!" she squealed, pointing at the screen.

Annie was right. *The Wizard of Oz* was perfect family fare with just enough excitement and drama, but with so much magic, love, and color. This was prime family quality time, but I didn't last long. The strong sleep aid was taking effect, and I was off to my own magic kingdom.

In a way, the timing was perfect: Judy was just launching into "Somewhere over the Rainbow" when I began drifting. Somehow, I was conscious that I wasn't awake. I knew I was slipping into deep, hard sleep—and I was gone.

There was smoke, heavy smoke; all my instincts were on high alert. My eyes watered, my nose ran, and I had a sick, nauseous feeling deep in my belly. I was there again even as part of me remained in our bedroom and aware that I was dreaming.

Slowly, the dream details sharpened, and I realized I was dressed in my full fire department turnout. In the flickering, smoky light, I could see my reflection against a shiny smooth wall. Helmet, boots, bunker pants—black with those shiny yellow stripes—all my gear was on. The jacket and gloves were heavy and awkward, but the only protection I could take with me when I faced a fire. The wall before me was polished as smooth as a mirror. That's how I knew what I was wearing. I stepped closer. It looked like marble, and it flickered in the light coming in from the hallway. It was a strange living light even though the smoke hid the ceiling. I saw through the smoke a corridor of some kind, leading to an opening back in the rear. *Where am I?* Then I saw the elevator. That gave it away. I was in the lobby of the North Tower once again. I was alone.

The elevator door kept opening part way and then closing as if something was blocking it and keeping it from going to its next call. But I couldn't see anything from where I stood, and it automatically continued to open and close.

I decided to investigate the mysterious opening down in the rear, and there I saw a burning pond, a low-level fire. Thick black smoke coiled off the burning pond, clinging to my eyes and nose and leaving a harsh metallic taste in my mouth. I don't know how, but I knew the pond was jet fuel and not water, and I realized it was stretched out across Austin Tobin Plaza. There was something else in the middle of the pond, but I couldn't make it out. It looked like two recliners stuck together. *Two recliners in the middle of a pond of jet fuel covering the plaza?* Careful of the flames and the smoke, I moved closer to try to see what the objects were and to get a better view of the spreading lake of fire, but something inside of me pushed me back. *Not today, pal. Not today,* said the voice inside my head.

I turned around and made my way down the hall to the smoke-filled lobby. Suddenly, I sensed movement. When dressed in full gear, a firefighter's peripheral vision is limited, but after years on the job, you learn to sense such things. There was something approaching on my right blind side. It was a tall, lanky man in a floppy hat with a sack over his head that had cutouts only for his eyes, nose, and mouth. Despite the strange headgear, he had on a black and yellow fireman's jacket with the collar turned up. Something about his movement was off—a little awkward and jerky—and I could see straw sticking out over his collar; from the gaps in the jacket front, where it clasped shut; and from just about everywhere else.

He came up to me and looked me in the eyes.

"There's no time to dilly dally! There's no time," he said.

"What the hell are you supposed to be?" I demanded.

Even for a dream, this wasn't making sense.

"Why, I'm your worst nightmare." Despite his troubling words, his voice was calm and commanding. "Don't you recognize me?" He put both hands on his hips. "*Your* head isn't made out of straw, is it? We haven't much time!" He waved his straw-stuffed glove and pointed one bumpy hay-filled finger toward the North Tower stairwell.

Then he took off ahead of me, climbing the stairs in his awkward scarecrow manner and leaving small piles of hay with each step. Losing straw like that made every step seem as if it might be his last. He climbed, and I followed. Still vaguely aware that I was in a dream,

I didn't try to wake up. (Later, my wife told me that my legs moved during my sleep as if I were marching—or climbing.)

We continued up, up, up, and up several flights through those smoky stairwells. Then he stopped on a landing and turned toward me.

"Hush! Do you hear that?"

The sound was familiar, too familiar. A sound only a firefighter would recognize from that distance. It was metal on metal—an ax hitting a halligan with halligan driving the its beveled edge deep. The sound tools make during the forced entry into a burning building. On the landing I noticed another firefighter, or what seemed to be a firefighter—he was wearing a fireman's jacket—and he was swinging a silver ax. Maybe that was when I realized that the firefighter on the landing wasn't just swinging a silver ax—*he* was silver or at any rate metallic. He was the Tin Man, complete with a shiny funnel cap on his head!

He swung his ax with the controlled urgency and skill of a dedicated fireman. I was breathless from the climb and from the shock of seeing this Tin Man firefighter.

"Ho! Ho! Hold up!" I stopped him with my command, putting a hand on his shoulder to halt his next swing. "Is there someone behind that wall that needs saving?"

"Oh, there's always someone somewhere that needs help," he replied politely. "That is, if you've got the heart to help them." Then he turned back to the task at hand. "May I get you to reposition my halligan?"

The halligan was already wedged into the landing door, ready for the next blow of his ax. But before any of us could make another move, we heard a rumble. From some distance—I estimate a couple of floors above us—I heard a familiar voice.

"Daddy! Daddy!" echoed the tiny voice in the stairwell.

I gasped. *No! It couldn't be!* But there was no denying it: It was the distinctive cry of my daughter, my own Tara.

Suddenly the building shuddered with a massive jolt that brought the three of us to our knees. We heard heavy footsteps thudding down the stairs toward us. Looking down at us from the landing above was another firefighter—a lion, standing upright and wearing the same jacket we had on. He had my daughter, Tara, in his huge paws and held her above his huge tawny head and great shaggy mane.

"I'm afraid! I'm afraid!" It wasn't my daughter calling out. It was the lion.

"Come down here, Lion," ordered the Scarecrow, and the Lion took the last steps down the North Tower stairs to our landing and handed me my daughter.

Tara was wearing her white christening gown and cap; in her tiny hands she held tight to her grandmother's Celtic cross. I clasped her to me, still unable to believe she was there, and I felt the soft bulk of her body and took in the sweet milky smell of her breath. She buried her head in my chest and snuggled deeper into my arms.

"It'll be okay, honey," I whispered into her curls. "Daddy is just sleeping."

I looked up at the Lion and saw that his eyes were squinting and his whiskers trembled. He was nearly in tears as I thanked him. I kept my voice low for both the sake of my daughter and this great cowardly beast.

"I was scared! I was scared," he confessed in a tone equally quiet and meek.

"There, there now, Lion." The Scarecrow stepped forward and reached up to dry the tears that leaked down the golden brown chest of hair. "There's no reason to be afraid. You're among friends, and you've done a fine job."

The Scarecrow spoke with certainty, but the night wasn't over. Just then without warning, the giant megastructure began to shake and tremble.

"Daddy!" Tara cried and wailed as only a terrified child could.

In response, the Scarecrow reached over and wrapped his straw-filled arms around us both, shielding the child in my arms and me. Behind us, the Tin Man lifted his ax, getting ready to swing it, and the Lion extended his claws, preparing to strike. The lion then let out a great resounding roar designed to inspire both his courage and our own, but as he roared, the darkness fell.

*   *   *

I rolled out of bed and onto the soft bedroom carpet to see my surprised wife peeking down at me from above. I was lucky to fall when I did and onto the soft carpet and out of the surreal, terrifying darkness of that dream. It was a fall, yes, but a safe one.

(Annie told me that I had sat up in bed the moment before rolling over. Eyes wide open, I had said, "There's no place like home!" I believe her, but I have no recollection of that.)

What I remembered—of the dream and of my daughter—still had me in its grip.

"Where's the baby?" I demanded, throwing on my robe and tying it in a huff.

"I brought her into her crib when it looked like you started having a little nightmare," Annie, still calm, replied.

"To me, Annie, that was no *little* nightmare."

I was barking at her, and I knew it but part of me was still back in that building with my odd companions and my daughter. I grabbed my walking cane, checked on the baby, and stumped downstairs. My journal was waiting for me, and I sat at the kitchen table, writing furiously to capture the bizarre images from my dream. I couldn't remember any dream that had ever felt so real. It was clear something was trying to break through my battered defenses. Although it was terrifying, it was also exciting—a literal breakthrough! Somehow between the medication and the movie, I had tapped into some part of myself, some well of memory and emotion that I had never been able to explore. The stress was falling off of me as I wrote. Even the horror of the dream and of Tara's cry began melting away in my joy at this development.

"Are you all right, George?"

I hadn't even heard Annie come down behind me. Now she stood behind me in the kitchen, watching me with concern.

"I'm all right, Irish, but the dream was out of this world," I told her. "Tara was in it, babe."

I put down my pen to recount the details to her. As the rush of words flowed out, I must have sounded like a mad man, but I didn't care.

"She was wearing her christening gown and that little hat. And she was holding that ancient Celtic cross. You know, the one over her crib? The one that Grandma gave her?"

"Well, I think I can solve one mystery for you." Annie was smiling now, as she settled into a kitchen chair beside me. "Maybe you don't even remember. But about one week before—you know …" Annie paused for a moment unsure of her words but then rallied, "about one week before 9/11, we had our christening for Tara up at the church. Given your work schedule and everything, that was probably one of the last times you spent any time with her before you got hurt."

"Good point!" I felt like a mad analyst, making connections everywhere. "I'll make a note of it."

I wrote on, furiously, desperate to get it all out onto the paper, make clear the connections, and record the flood of emotions that the dream had provoked. Annie's vivid memories of her late mother made it seem as if "Bridie" was with us today.

Annie's mother Bridget Boland, otherwise known as Bridie, had been the neighborhood centerpiece in her day. In the late 1950s and early 1960s, when families could leave the screen door open or not worry about the kids playing in front of the house, Bridie had grown to the status of neighborhood mayor. Everyone who knew and met her—including her large family—had loved her. She had her wonderful husband, Thomas Tobin, a retired army engineer; their two handsome sons; and their three pretty and vivacious daughters, one of which was my loving Annie. Life and family were good even until its finale. On Bridie's sick bed in St. Vincent's Hospital in 1984, the family had marched in one by one to see and share time with their ailing mother. Annie had been the last to arrive due to her new assignment as a nurse to the fire department's medical division. Her mom had looked somewhat pale and weak when she had finally arrived. They'd had a short conversation and prayer, and then Bridie had spoken softly.

"Anne Marie, darling, I want you to have this." Bridie had said as she had unfolded some thin white tissue paper. From it she had lifted a small light gray cross, made of fine Irish porcelain and marked on its center with a Celtic design.

"It was given to my mother by your great-grandmother, which had been handed down from her mother long ago. Perchance the day will come when you have your own daughter. You might like to pass it along to her," Bridie had said gently in her Irish brogue as Annie's eyes swelled with tears.

It was a historic artifact of religion and nature used in the Crusades in the Celtic battles throughout the Middle Ages and earlier in wars around the globe.

Annie had placed it gently back on the tissue paper, folded it neatly and, holding the cross, given her mother a final kiss. After her mother had passed, Annie had kept the artifact stored away, occasionally taking a peek at it throughout the years to remind herself of her mother's wishes. In late August 2001, just a couple of weeks before 9/11, Annie had put the cross on our daughter's baby blanket during the christening ceremonies at the church. Tara Bridget Bachmann had received her grandmother's blessing and grandmother's name as her middle name. We took a family picture on the front steps of our Brooklyn brownstone later that day. It was the last happy moment I remembered before that horrifying day of destruction. Annie had hung the cross on the wall over the baby's crib, so her visiting brothers and sisters and other family members and friends could view it to witness the miracle and well-kept promise.

All of this I recorded in the journal. Finally, after writing for several minutes, I slowed down. I was exhausted, and with the fatigue came depression.

Mr. and Mrs. Bachmann with their daughter Tara, one week before 9/11

"You know, Irish, it would be a shame if after Vietnam, Cambodia, and twenty-seven-and-a-half years of fighting fires—not to mention my chance survival of September 11—if in the process of healing, I went and lost my mind."

Annie reached out to comfort me.

"Tara and I will take care of you, Daddy," she said, her voice soft and loving.

We held each other in the darkness of the brownstone's kitchen until I had calmed enough to finish the night's task. When I felt I could, I pulled away from her gently, and she watched as I wrote down the last of my dream and the odd connections and memories it had raised.

Once finished, Annie helped me to my feet and upstairs. Together, we checked in on Tara, snoring with those gentle little snores only a baby can make, and then we climbed back into our own bed.

CHAPTER 7
E.T. Within Quadrant 1

That dream and the drama of remembering it, writing it out, and drawing connections left me feeling purged somehow. It was as if something poisonous had been drained from me. In my mind at least, I was myself again. In my body, I still had problems galore and found myself working full time just to keep up my doctor's appointments in various offices, and the at-home physical therapy with which Annie helped to keep my healing on track.

Then there was the paperwork. Before I could officially retire from the New York City Fire Department, I had to have my injuries evaluated to assess my disability level. What a joke! But forms are forms and clerks are clerks. And so I went on the rounds, submitting myself to all of the poking and prodding. The herd—doctors, nurses, and specialists of all sorts—went over me from head to toe. They even went beyond my 9/11 injuries and inquired about the dual strains of malaria, one of which was a killer that I've carried in my blood since my tour in Vietnam. I actually picked the bad one up in Cambodia when I had been spearheading operations for the First Air Cavalry Division in 1970. The malaria tablets I had taken regularly had been no help.

The killer strain had come to Cambodia by way of India. Female mosquitoes, one of which found me, had carried it to Cambodia's hot, wet jungles. The tricky thing about malaria is, of course, that there is no cure. Once bitten, you are stung for life. From then on I had been obligated to reveal forever on every health exam or to anyone who wanted to take my blood that I have really bad malaria.

I was idealistic. I was a kid who had dropped out of high school and signed up for reasons that had made sense at the time. High school hadn't been for me. I spent what could have been my prom night on the Ho Chi Minh Trail. At nineteen, I was a paratrooper with the Eighty-Second Airborne in Fort Bragg, North Carolina. For a while with the Cambodia operation, I carried a flamethrower, "The Dragon's Breath" we called it affectionately. We were supposed to use it as a tool—not a weapon. We were trained to use it to destroy any logistical information or supplies that we captured from the enemy.

Some images will never leave me, like the mind-blowing vision of Communist North Vietnamese soldiers running down trails through the pitch black of the primordial jungle and then being lit up by my buddies and me by that bright, wet flame. The images recur, thanks to post-traumatic stress disorder (PTSD) and Uncle Sam's "Dragon's Breath." That was one reason I wanted to become a firefighter. At least about that decision, I have no regrets.

Thanks to all the shrapnel in me since that war, MRIs were off-limits as I made my rounds through doctors and insurance men. Instead, they made do with other tools—measuring and testing me with CAT scans, myelograms, and X-rays. Honestly, I think my body was already pretty well chewed up before 9/11 from nearly three decades worth of front line firefighting. But they went ahead, measuring, peering, testing, and gaping. Here I was, the survivor—Vietnam, Cambodia, and, for a glorious finale, 9/11 by a mere fluke of fate.

Despite that first breakthrough, it wasn't the cheeriest time, and the constant back and forth began to weigh on me. We, as a department, were burying our dead. I couldn't make every funeral as much as I would have liked to, but I went whenever I could. And although I couldn't yet remember what had happened to me on 9/11, I did—we did as a family—begin to make some recovery and some headway toward healing. Annie and Tara supplied faith when I lagged and kept me going. But there was still so much left to do. That first breakthrough had seemed so easy in retrospect, but it was only the first step on a very long path. But we are made to endure, and we are sustained by both faith and love. Given the slightest chance of survival, the human mind works to heal itself. Between the drudgery, the sadness, my frustration, and the constant support from Annie, I knew what had to happen long before I admitted it to myself: Once again, the time had come for me to take a step. It was time again for me to face my nightmares.

Seventh Heaven runs along Seventh Avenue in Park Slope, Brooklyn. Seventh Heaven is a street fair and usually falls on the third Sunday in June. It's just like every other street fair in the city, except of course it's ours. From blocks away, you can smell the sausages and peppers cooking, ready to burst open and be scooped up onto bulky rolls. The sugar from the cotton candy machine adds sweetness to the spice, and everyone, every ethnic group and all ages, is out on the street. They should be; there is something for everyone there: a classic car showcase for auto enthusiasts, fruit crêpes for sweet tooths, rides for the kids, and politicians side by side with balloon-twisting clowns for the children. Add a soundtrack of high-decibel rock 'n' roll, and it's a street fair. It's summer in the city, and nowhere else compares.

After tucking Tara into her three-wheeled baby jogger, we hit the street. There were people to see, treats to sample, and all sorts of souvenirs to buy and carry. It was hot already, but everyone was out, and we saw neighbors and old friends, folks we hadn't seen in ages and whose joyful faces made 9/11 seem like a bad and distant dream. I didn't want to go back; this was life. This was too much fun.

I'd paid my dues according to my own survivor's guilt by attending every funeral and memorial service that I could until my heart could stand no more. What complicated things of course was that I still had no memory of how I had survived—of what I might feel guilty about. *I know I was there. But why? How?* I had no idea. The only clues came in the form of thumping headaches, which laid me out and forced me off my feet. There was a mystery still buried someplace in my mind, and every now and then, that mystery fought to surface.

The day went on as such days do, and finally when we'd eaten all our snacks and said hi to all our neighbors, I realized that it was getting a little bit cool. The late afternoon light was giving way to evening, and the crowds had started to thin. Vendors who'd been busy only a short while ago set about disassembling their booths and putting away the day's delights. The sanitation department began its slow sweep up the street, and our own local police began to collect the blue wooden crowd barriers.

Wiped out from the day's fun, Annie, Tara, and I took refuge in our neighborhood Mexican restaurant. The young owner, Joe, recognized us and sent over a round of drinks. Joe had contributed food to the workers at Ground Zero in those early horrible days after the attacks. His restaurant has become a regular spot for us, and that night we had a light dinner, lingering until the last spring twilight was gone. As we headed home the sky was a blanket of stars. It was a perfect night, and we strolled back toward home. But the day didn't end without one more surprise.

"Daddy! Guess what?" Annie said, turning to face me. "Mommy got you and baby a big surprise! While you and baby were checking out the classic cars, Mommy sneaked over to the Video Shack and got *E.T.*"

E.T., Stephen Spielberg's 1982 science fiction film chronicling the adventures of a lost alien, had been recently re-released. By March 2002, six months after 9/11, the DVD and video of the film were available at every Blockbuster and mom and pop video store in the country. The re-release had spurred a flood of stories about the family classic. One story reported that Spielberg had created the visuals of the little alien from interviews with people who were supposedly abducted by UFOs. From these interviews, he'd put together the hairless little creature, complete with his powers of telekinesis and that glowing index finger by which he could levitate objects and rejuvenate life.

First we had attended the fair, which was to be followed by a wonderful, family video? Annie's surprise seemed like a great idea. Of course, I didn't know then that it would spark another nightmare, almost as realistic and horrifying as the first.

After we reached home, we each settled in. Annie tapped away at her computer and chatted with her sister and good friend Kathy on the phone. Tara and I made our way upstairs and started the movie, knowing that Annie would join us soon. Right from the beginning, Tara was entranced. The little alien wasn't the scary kind; in fact, he seemed more like a pet or another baby. While I massaged Tara's back and legs, she stared at the screen as the human boy, Elliott, befriended the delicate space visitor. Everything seemed so peaceful and under control, and I felt calm. The day had been a success. But ...

Annie had been urging me to continue my sleep therapy. So while Tara stared at the images on the screen, I took another of Dr. Mahoney's sleeping pills, determined to bring my family even closer by healing my wounded mind. It wasn't long before Tara drifted off into the peaceful sleep of the young. I, however, was headed somewhere else.

Seemingly half awake, my vision blurred, and I found myself lying on a surface of white pulverized ash. I could taste the acrid dryness and hear the rumbling clouds passing above me. Lying on my side, I looked up, and recognized the façade and the buildings. I was on West Street again. One eye was open, and I could see the smoke, but I couldn't move and my breathing was limited. Something was weighing me down, something heavy and immovable.

Slowly, time passed, and the dark smoke cleared a little. I realized that I was pinned under a giant T-bar of steel, what seemed like a steel girder. *How did get here? How will I ever get out?* I was wearing my fire gear: my jacket and pants—but no helmet.

"Where the fuck is my helmet?" I asked out loud.

Then in the distance, I saw movement. It was something white, and it was getting closer. Strolling across the wreckage and coming out of the dense, dark smoke, it was my baby. It was my Tara, and she was dressed in her christening gown with her grandmother's Celtic cross held tightly in her chubby hand.

"Tara! Tara!" I yelled and heard my voice reverberate and echo.

We were truly in a wasteland, but she kept coming toward me, so sweet and so pure. And it hit me: I was ashamed. *I have degenerated into this helpless thing, barely grasping for survival and pinned like an insect. I don't want her to see me like this.* But she ran toward to where I was underneath the steel girder.

"Daddy, Daddy!" Her little baby voice brought tears to my eyes. "Daddy, why are you under there?"

My tears turned to rage. *Why does she have to see me like this? Why? Damn it. Why?* She got down on her knees with her white dress pressing into the dirty ash and tried to snuggle up against me. Her gown was getting dirty, and there was nothing I could do about it.

"It's okay, baby." I tried to sound comforting. "Mommy will wake us up soon."

I could feel my eyes and nose running, and I knew that it wasn't just the ash getting to me. Just then, I felt a breeze. The wind had picked up, and looking beyond Tara, I could see it beginning to swirl. First like a dust devil, the ash rose in a narrow coil and then became more like a small tornado, growing into an immense and powerful wind. Pieces of paper swirled above us an were picked up by the growing squall. As I watched, sparks seemed to fly in my memory. *I am supposed to see this. But why?* There was something on the edge of my mind. Something was starting to click.

I reached out with my one free hand while still holding onto Tara. The whirlwind continued to gather strength. I couldn't lift my head, and I held her tight. Something big was approaching. Something or someone.

"Look Da! Look! The space boy! E.T.!" Tara screamed.

Is she screaming out of fear—or excitement?

"Daddy, look! E.T.!"

I blinked away the ash. Lo and behold, she was right: A giant version of Spielberg's Extraterrestrial was standing there. It must have been two stories high, towering over us with its brown bubbling skin. Its large head bent toward us; its huge eyes and slit mouth came closer on that weird, retractable neck. Its head tilted to one side, like a curious puppy. Tara wiggled out of my grip, and I started to panic.

"Tara! Tara! Come back to me! Come to Daddy!"

She'd gone for a closer look, and I couldn't do anything. I was pinned, and she was already about twenty feet away, standing in an ash-covered moonscape and looking up at the two-story monster. The monster seemed to smile at her, or maybe he was looking at the Celtic cross that she was still holding. For some reason, it seemed like they were communicating. But then the massive beast moved and reached out one giant arm toward her.

"No, no, you bastard! She's just a baby!" I cried out, helpless in my state. "Don't you hurt her!"

They didn't seem to notice my distress, but suddenly his giant finger started to glow. A red glow lit up the landscape, warming the dead gray ash. I found myself calming down and noticed that the girder that had had me pinned seemed to be moving. *Impossible,* I thought. *It has to weigh several tons, but there is no denying it.* The girder was rising, levitating in the red glow of that pointed brown finger. It lifted off me, and I was freed. I sat up, and Tara came running back.

"Da! Da! E.T. did it! E.T.!"

Amazingly, I was not injured in my dream. Still, I was cautious, and I got up slowly, a step at a time. Once on my feet, I took little Tara's hand and walked toward the creature, the giant alien who had saved me. We stood before the alien, and behind us, the girder came crashing back down. The two-story alien bent down to look at us closer. Leaning forward, E.T. began to extend its neck higher and higher. Although his mouth never seemed to move, I heard a high-pitched and creaky voice, like an old man's, call out two words.

"Be good!"

Tara was enthralled, and I no longer knew what to think. Then the alien stood up straight and lifted his right hand to cup the top of his right eye. *I'll be damned if it isn't saluting us!*

I looked down at my daughter with her hand still in mine.

She turned to me and asked, "Da, can we go home now?"

I woke next to Tara, laughing and crying at the same time. *What is with these crazy dreams? Am I cursed to have these fucking dreams for the rest of my life? What is going on? Is this survivor's guilt or 9/11 post-traumatic stress? I have to know; I have to find out.*

I made my way downstairs, determined to tell Annie. *How long had I been asleep?* She was still on the phone, so I grabbed a pencil and began to write, determined to capture the vision in Dr. Mahoney's dream journal before its incredible realism faded from my memory.

The vividness of the dream had surprised me. I was dreaming in three-dimensional Technicolor Sensurround even. Great production quality for a dream! I hadn't had too much experience with dreams or dream analysis at that point. In retrospect, I had had some doozies, even before 9/11. Vietnam, and all the baggage after my tour there, had certainly provoked some nightmares that had lingered, and I'd spent time with a Veteran's Administration therapist on my way back to sanity. But basically, those dreams had faded, especially once I had promised the therapist that I'd stay away from such evocative movies as *Apocalypse Now, Platoon,* and *Hamburger Hill.* Now, the dreams were more wild, vivid, and real. And all I was watching were kids' movies, films designed as much for Tara as for Annie and me.

I felt I was headed down a path into some dark place where I couldn't see. If there were signposts, I couldn't read them. If there were steps, I didn't see them. All I knew was that my dreams had something to do with what had happened to me that fateful Tuesday morning. And I knew I had to continue down that path, working every way I could to remember what had happened in order to fully heal—for my family and for myself.

Sleepy time for Tara Bridget

Chapter 8
Nemo and the Big Fall

My skepticism regarding dream therapy was beginning to crumble. As horrible as they were, the nightmares had done something for me. I felt a release of pressure as if some of the pain of that horrible day had been discharged, like some noxious gas, through my dreams' crazy images. I was feeling a little bit better. I had my wife and daughter. We were all alive and, more or less, well.

The rest of the country was still reeling. Television reports and newspapers were awash with horrible images, the repeating images of the towers coming down and the reality of body recovery and identifications. The radio stations broadcast human interest stories, telling of some unfortunate child who had been orphaned in the attacks and was crying him- or herself to sleep. My country was crying.

I was keeping another notebook now for Mrs. Miller, the grief counselor. In this one, I was recording my waking thoughts, as in what was hard for me, what provoked memories or emotional responses, and what made me think. In it I wrote that I had come to the time of what I referred to as "the pressure phone calls."

The first of these started off well. It was from my fellow firefighter and buddy, John Moribito. Another survivor from the Ten House, John had served with Ladder 10 and was known as "the hero chauffeur." He'd driven the ladder company truck closest to Ground Zero, and as the chauffeur his job was to stay with the truck and respond to the radio. But he had been a hero before that—the recipient of numerous citations even before that day. He'd called to tell me that my helmet had been found in the ruins on West Street. They were holding it for me at the temporary Ten House across the South Street Seaport.

It felt odd to call another firehouse Ten House, but I understood the relocation. At that point in the summer of 2002, Ten House, the only firehouse to sustain structural damage on 9/11, was being used as a staging area for Ground Zero workers, so both Ladder 10 and Engine 10 had been temporarily relocated. Later under Mayor Michael Bloomberg the city restored our home-away-from-home on Liberty Street, not only repairing the decimated firehouse, but also replacing our beloved rigs with state-of-the-art engine and fire truck.

I hobbled down to the South Street Seaport, where I was presented with my burnt and blackened helmet. It had been encased in a see-through display case as if it were some priceless relic or work of art. To me, it looked like a helmet—*my* helmet. Only in addition to the fire damage, it had been squashed and tilted as if something had smashed it hard from the side.

Captain Engle made a little speech as he handed it to me.

"Now, George," he said, "here is a little token that will help when you tell 9/11 war stories to your grandchildren."

"Thanks, Cap!" I replied with a grin, wanting to keep the tone light and the mood celebratory. "I'm just glad my head isn't still in it!"

With all we'd all been through, my comment hit the right note. A low roar of laughter broke out from the firefighters gathered around.

All in all, things seemed to be a getting better all the time. Despite my injuries, I was beginning to miss the warm physical relationship Annie and I had once enjoyed. Yes, my back was still in bad shape, but I thought I was ready.

"Now, Irish," I stated making my case one night, "Mayor Giuliani says we should continue on with our lives as if nothing has happened. Otherwise, the damned terrorists have won."

She wasn't buying it.

"Are you kidding me?" she snapped back. "What about your friggin' back, your burns, and your head? Don't even think about it!"

For the near future at any rate, the terrorists were up one.

Still, I began to feel that maybe the worst was over. I'd tried the sleep medication again, sleeping in a separate room of our brownstone so as not to disturb Annie and little Tara with my wild nightmares. But without their presence and the visual cues of a movie playing, my sleep was just that: deep, dark, and sound.

About a week later, I intercepted a phone call from Dr. Mahoney. He was trying to reach Annie for an update and wanted to know if my amnesia was letting up at all. When I reported that I had glimmers but nothing resembling a whole memory yet, he hit me with another suggestion: hypnotherapy.

I balked. I'd seen too many stories about guys going into a trance. I could *just barely* deal with nightmares. Nobody was going to "put me under." I immediately turned him down, trying to soften my rejection by pointing out that although I'd never been put in a trance, I figured it probably wouldn't work on me anyway.

Was I being stubborn? Maybe. But it had been months by that point. I was sick of doctors, of doctors' offices, and doctors' appointments. Maybe I knew that I would give in. Maybe I knew I was just stalling for time, but for now the issue was closed. I wasn't going to let myself be hypnotized.

Dr. Mahoney must have heard the frustration in my voice. Maybe he also picked up my resistance as just that—resistance. He backed off, telling me he'd check in again in another week. In the meantime, he reminded me that I should definitely keep seeing Mrs. Miller. As we hung up, I knew that if he reached Annie on his next check-in phone call, I was in trouble. There would be no more stalling.

In the meantime, I had other things on my mind. The mother of all pressure phone calls had come in. It was official. It was some suit calling, speaking for the top brass at the New York City Fire Department, and ordering me to testify for the 9/11 Commission. The hearings were being held at No. 9 Metro Tech, the department's headquarters. I was to be subpoenaed and sworn in and then to testify before the commission panel. The caller briefed me, giving me the specifics. I was to show up in ten days, wearing my Class A dress uniform. The subpoena would follow in the mail.

"Why me?" I finally got up the nerve to ask.

"Because of where you were found," the suit told me.

According to the department's virtual map, I had been rescued and my helmet had been found in the proximity of the command post's remains on West Street in Quadrant 1.

"That's why. They wanna know what you saw," the suit told me.

"Yes, sir," I told him and then hung up.

The fuse was lit. The clock was ticking. I had ten days and a thumping headache. That was it. The dilemma facing us was pretty obvious. If I didn't regain my memory in ten days, I risked my disability from the department and 9/11 compensation. I had ten days to dredge up the horrors and retrieve those hours that I'd been suppressing since the day itself.

And it wasn't just about the money; although God knows, we'd needed it. No, this was about something much bigger. In ten days, I would be called to bear witness, and I took this very seriously. I certainly wasn't going to lie about the honored dead. I had ten days, and I needed to know what had happened.

Annie, ever practical, wanted to call Dr. Mahoney right away.

"We'll make a hypnotherapy appointment for you. The first one available," she said. "It's worth a shot."

But the idea scared me. I'd lost so much and was beginning to regain some of my old self—physically and mentally. *How can I let someone else take over my mind?*

"Please, Annie, let me think on it. Just overnight?"

"Okay, okay," she agreed. She knew how stubborn I could get. "We'll sleep on it."

I knew this was her strategy. She suggested an idea, and if I disagreed, she allowed me to get use to it. That was fine by me. I was buying time, any time I could.

"Let's give it 'til next week," I suggested.

With a resigned sigh, she agreed.

I could tell Annie was a nervous wreck over the weekend, but she didn't talk to me about it. I knew what she wanted me to do, and she knew how scared I was. Instead, I watched as she jabber-jabbered over the phone, tying up the line to her sisters, her girlfriends from work, and all of her buddies, and the constant sound of her talking—talking to everyone else except me—began to drive me around the bend. In retrospect, I think we were both panicked by our situation. We were facing a big deadline, and the only way either of us could see to clear it was for me to give up control of my mind. There was so much at risk no matter which way we went, and the pressure was getting to us both. I could tell.

By Sunday, I needed a distraction. I needed to get away from the house, Annie, and her endless conversations with everyone but me. Luckily, the weather was fine, and so I took baby Tara out for a long walk. Loading up the baby jogger with a bottle of water for me and some crackers and juice for Tara, we set out for Prospect Park. I carried an emergency quick-change outfit for Tara, just in case. Although we intended to make a day of it, I was actually the one who gave in first. Between the growing summer heat and my healing back, the combination of stroller and swings was just too much. Within a few hours, my head was exploding, and my back was demanding that I give up and lie down.

We made our way home from the park by Union Street as a father and child both hungry and tired. Annie had gone shopping with one of her sisters, so the house was empty and quiet. After lunch, Tara and I were both ready for a nap. As I took us both up to the big bedroom, I saw the early summer sky turning dark. We were in for a storm.

Just then Annie called. The weather had gotten to her, too. She was cutting short the shopping excursion.

"I'll be home in an hour or two," she told me.

When I told her how we'd spent our morning and how my back was acting up, she suggested, "Why don't you lay down with the baby? Throw on a video." As an afterthought, she added, "Nothing scary now! And if you can't sleep take one of those big blue pills."

"Okay, Mommy! Okay!" I was tired enough to let myself be bullied a bit. Besides, her advice made sense. "Everything will be just fine. Mind the traffic on your way home."

The rain started to hit the window the moment I hung up, and a sudden rumble in the sky spooked Tara.

"Let's watch a video, Tara!" I picked her up, hoping to distract her from the growing thunder and placed her in a cocoon of pillows on the bed. "What do you feel like watching today?"

I browsed through our modest video collection. The bald, green, smiling face of Shrek stared out at me.

"No, I don't think so." I didn't want to imagine what kind of dreams that face could conjure up. "Let's find something more benign."

Finally, I threw another tape into the machine without much further thought. It wasn't at the beginning, but I didn't rewind it. I tried to find a comfortable position for my back. Tara had snuggled in beside me.

"I love you, Da," she whispered, before falling asleep.

It had seemed like a good idea to lie down, but my back was still not quite right, so I slipped away to the bathroom, where I downed one of those big blue horse pills. A nap would do us both good.

By the time I'd tiptoed back into the bedroom and slipped in next to Tara, the movie was well underway. On the screen, there was an animated clownfish searching for his lost child, somewhere off of the coast of Australia. It was Disney at its best.

Just then the sky cracked open with a horrendous boom. Tara slept through it, calm as ever, but it sure made me jump! The whole concept seemed funny, as otherworldly as those neon fish with their almost human faces. *What did I have to be scared of?* I thought as I faded into the intense drugged dreamtime of those big, blue pills. *Why should I be scared of anything anymore?*

Never take anything for granted: I woke up, as was becoming usual for me, inside a dream. I was sitting this time with my legs crossed in the lotus position. Looking up, I saw a clear, blue sky, and there was a hard wind that blew strong and constant from one direction. The loud *thump thump thump* of a helicopter's blade grew louder until the chopper itself appeared, hovering overhead. On its side were the letters *NYPD*. I had no idea where I was.

I tried to untangle my legs to get up, and I realized that I was again dressed in my full firefighting gear. I moved my boot and heard a funny sound, like the hard rubber sole moving over pebbles—or, no, more like gravel. I was sitting on gravel. *But where am I?*

Suddenly, my sense of smell was aroused. The air was thick and dark with jet fuel.

"Oh, God!" I screamed silently in my dream voice.

I then noticed that not too far from where I sat there appeared to be a shed dwarfed by an immense antenna in the middle of the field of gravel. I was on the roof of the North Tower. *Move!* my mind screamed. I knew what was to come. As I untangled my legs and scrambled to my feet, something touched my back, startling me. I turned and looked down. To my shock and panic, Tara was again with me in her white christening gown and matching lace cap. She had touched me. Her arms were stretched out toward me, and in her chubby hands she held her grandmother's Celtic cross.

"Da!" she cried out. "Da! Where's Mommy?"

"It's okay, baby. Daddy's here with you." I bent down to take her in my arms. In my gentlest fatherly voice, I whispered to her assuringly, "It's okay, Tara. Mommy will wake us up soon, baby. I promise." I was trying to comfort her—to comfort myself. I wanted to believe what I was saying. "She'll be here soon. I promise."

I lifted my little angel in her white dress and held her close against my heavy firefighter's coat. As I contemplated what to do next, the building began to buckle and jolt. Still holding her, I fell to one knee. I realized I could see into a police chopper above us. Inside, the pilot was saluting us.

For a moment, I felt cheery. *We'll be rescued!* My heart leapt at the thought, but then the unavoidable reality came from deep down in my belly. It came at me with the certainty of instinct, of gut knowledge. *Nobody ever gets rescued from anything this bad.*

The sound of twisting metal was a scream with no end. A million car accidents happened, slowly, beneath us. I held Tara to me, tightly, opening up my turnout jacket to pull her closer and shield her from what was to come. She was half inside my firefighter's jacket, and I could feel the warmth of her near my skin. I was glad she couldn't see my face flushed with fear. The antenna came corkscrewing down. The devastating process of a skyscraper's collapse had begun. The inevitable was happening now.

I ran to the edge of the roof and, without looking, stepped off. The smoke was getting thicker now, but I didn't look down.

"It's all right, baby." Tara started to cry, and I held her closer still. "We'll be home soon."

We fell so fast, and everything around us became white and blurry. Tumbling and twirling in the air, I lost my inner compass—unable to tell which way was up or even which way we were moving. The wind ripped Tara's cross out of her hand. She was sobbing and I tried to reassure her.

"That's all right, baby. We'll wake up soon. I promise."

As we continued our fall, I saw what appeared to be debris, orange debris, in the distance.

The object began to assume a more definite shape. It was definitely orange and round. Then I noticed its white and black stripes. It looked like a fish although I dismissed the thought as a product of my disorientation. But Tara saw it, too.

"Nemo, Daddy, Nemo!"

She was right. A great orange clownfish the size of a Saint Bernard had flown up beside and spoke to us directly in a little boy's voice. *Why not?* I thought to myself. *Nothing about any of this has been normal.*

"Don't be afraid, Tara," assured the fish, its feelings for my daughter evident in its large dark, sensitive eyes. "It's okay. All will be right now."

Tara held out her tiny hand, and the great fish touched it with its fin. Tara held onto Nemo's fin, and they both smiled as we sailed through the air.

The fish looked at me with those same soulful eyes.

"My father said I couldn't do these things," it told me. "He said I couldn't do these things. But I had to reach out—and so should you."

I considered the message in the fish's simple statement. Tara had let go of its fin now and in her hand was her grandmother's cross. The ground seemed closer.

"Good-bye, Tara! Good-bye!" the fish called back as it sailed away into the distance.

"Nemo, Da! Nemo!" Tara yelled in delight as we continued falling.

The ringing telephone beside our bed woke me. It was Annie. She was downstairs at the back door, calling me to help her with the groceries. I climbed out of bed, groggy from my dream, and lumbered downstairs, switching off our security system to rescue my wife from the soaking rain. Her arms were full.

"Is the baby sleeping?" she asked as she handed me a bag.

"Yes, here. Let me take the other ones," referring to the bags she was still balancing.

As we put our groceries away in the kitchen, I shook away the last of the medicated sleep.

"I had another wacky dream, Annie," I said and sat to record it in my journal.

"Hopefully, that will be the last of those dreams," said Annie, looking over at me.

She knew the dreams had been useful. They were the keys to getting my memory back, but she also knew the toll they took on me and how I was exhausted and moody for the days following.

"I've made an appointment with you to see the hypnotherapist on Tuesday," she continued. "We need to find another way for you to get your memory back."

"Jesus Christ, Anne! When were you going to tell me this?"

I was irritated. She shouldn't have sprung this on me now. Not when I'm fresh from—whatever it was.

"Is that why you wouldn't talk to me all weekend?"

Her silence confirmed my guess. She'd made the appointment, but she didn't want to ruin our weekend, so she did everything and anything *but* talk to me.

"For Christ's sake, why do I have to get hypnotized?"

I wasn't being rational, and I knew it. But I just didn't want to go back there to that place in my head.

"Don't you want to get better?" she snapped. "It might help you remember. It could make testifying a lot easier."

"Listen, Annie," I tried to explain. "Once I saw a nightclub act where a hypnotist had a group of men onstage and turned them into barnyard animals. He had them clucking and pecking at the ground like chickens. I don't like that shit." *Was she getting it?* I wanted her to understand. "I don't like the idea of someone doing that to me. I want to be in control. That's why when I go to the dentist, I never take gas no matter what they're drilling, I would rather get the Novocain and be awake, *be* present, *be* myself."

I was being defensive, I knew. But I explained myself as best as I

75

could. I thought I had made my case when Annie's face softened and she smiled at me.

"It will be okay, Daddy," she told me and reached out to touch my cheek with her soft hand. "When the hypnotherapist puts you under his trance, I'll make sure to bring extra chicken feed."

"Oh Christ, Irish!" I burst out laughing.

For this woman and our daughter, I'd do anything—even this.

CHAPTER 9
Reliving 9/11 through Hypnosis

The time to come to Jesus had all but arrived. The time for dreamtime to catch up with real time was in sight. The time had come to deal with what happened to me on September 11, 2001. I knew that no matter how opposed I was to hypnotherapy, if the only way to know what had happened was by relinquishing control to someone else, then it was time for the appointment.

God bless Annie for being able to move ahead when I was still paralyzed by fears, both rational and nonrational. She'd gotten the reference from our trusted Dr. Mahoney for an Upper West Side hypnotherapist, Joseph Lipinski. She did the homework for me, too, jotting down what Dr. Mahoney had told her and digging around a little on her own.

Dr. Lipinski was no quack, she was fast to reassure me. A world-renowned psychotherapist, he specialized in using hypnosis to help his patients and lectured around the world about his techniques. He'd written several books and worked out of practices in the United Kingdom and Canada, as well as Manhattan. He flew in from Canada to see me, all part of a team effort that focused on a particularly interesting and stubborn subject—the fact that I was that subject didn't make me feel any better.

The plan was pretty straightforward. As Annie and I bounced along in the cab through the Brooklyn Battery Tunnel, she and I went over everything. We were to meet Mrs. Miller, my grief counselor, at 11:00 a.m. in the lobby of Dr. Lipinski's building. Dr. Mahoney had explained to Annie how my attitude could determine whether Dr. Lipinski would be able to hypnotize me, and so she was doing her best to keep me calm and upbeat. With the cab jolting up and down, it wasn't easy.

"Does the babysitter have our cell phone number, Mommy?" I asked, nervous about everything.

"Yes, she does," replied Annie, trying to keep our collective cool. "I took care of everything."

I must have sighed or rolled my eyes because she gave me a look.

"George?"

"I'm sorry, Mommy. I'm not mad at you." Truth is, I wasn't, and I tried to explain. "I'm just mad that I have to go to some magician to help me recall the biggest nightmare of all time. I mean after all of the nightmare alleys I've run through?"

The cabbie sneaked a peek at me in his rearview mirror. We hit another pothole. It did not help.

"He's not a magician, George." Annie had on her calming-nurse manner as if I were one of her scared and wounded patients. Although I knew what she was trying to do, it was hard to accept what she was saying. "He's a world famous doctor, George. He specializes in this kind of trance-induced therapy. He's here to help you—to bring your memory back so you can stand up in front of the 9/11 Commission and testify." She took a deep breath and laid it out to me straight. "You need to do this for your sanity—and frankly, we need disability benefits. You earned them. And, you know, maybe most importantly, you need to do it for posterity. You have to bear witness to what you saw."

When she put it that way, I saw what a crybaby I was being. Good thing the cab was too small for her to send me off to stand in the corner!

"Okay, Annie, okay."

I nodded, agreeing to everything she'd said.

"You're supposed to be the bravest, so you'd better start acting like it!"

I couldn't even meet the cabbie's eyes in the rearview mirror, but I know he heard it all, and I felt appropriately ashamed.

We sat in silence for a while. Then we passed another firehouse. Milling about were fellow firefighters, all in dress uniforms. They were either going to or just returning from another funeral. It was all too close, too real. The side of my head began to throb. One of the last instructions we'd been given was no aspirin, Tylenol, or painkillers of any kind. I closed my eyes and tried to relax.

The cab pulled up to an Upper West Side residential building, the kind with apartments above and different professional offices below. The lovely Mrs. Miller was waiting for us in the lobby, and together we located Dr. Lipinski's name in the building directory. The three of us made our way to his large colorful suite of offices. They had a bit more personality than I'd expected from a shrink. A human skull sat on one shelf, a collection of alien-looking glass pyramids were lined up on his desk, and the picture on the back wall showed a smiling Sigmund Freud flipping the bird! *Maybe this guy is some kind of witch doctor after all.*

We were admitted to his inner office and stood waiting. It wasn't long before Lipinski joined us. Portly and dressed in a sharp gray sharkskin suit with a white open-collared shirt, he looked sophisticated but relaxed. His gray hair and goatee gave him a look of refinement, just what you'd expect a shrink to look like, and his Russian accent gave him a certain continental flair.

Once we'd introduced ourselves, he took charge.

"Please be seated," he said in his Boris Badenov accent. "George, please in the middle. Mrs. Miller and Mrs. Bachmann, please on each side."

We sat and waited for further instructions.

"Now, George," he continued but his accent made me scan the room for Rocky or Bullwinkle. "You must want to go back to that day in order for all this to work. That is key, yes?"

I looked around for my cartoon heroes, wondering if they'd been tied up in a closet and were in need of rescue.

"Yes, Dr. Lipinski." I gave up my fancy and focused on the doctor. "I'm all yours."

"Now, George, I need for you to follow a set of instructions that I am going to give you. You need to obey them without any question whatsoever."

This, along with my lingering concerns for a certain flying squirrel, was all too much.

"The problem, Doctor, is that I'm not sure if I'm the type of person who can be entranced. I mean I have a short attention span."

I revealed that last bit with nervous embarrassment as my last-ditch effort to avoid this entire trial. As soon as I said it, I could see out of the corner of my eye that Annie had her mad face on.

The doctor took no notice and continued on in his soothing voice, "I can assure you, George, if you relax and listen to me, we can get you back."

I was staring at his eyes, which were mesmerizing.

"We can take you back to that morning."

I don't have to agree. I am in his office, aren't I? I can leave anytime, can't I? But he began to give instructions.

"You will hear different voices," he said like he'd said it a million times before. "One voice will be the narrator, the main voice that will walk us through the events of that day. The other voice will be the commentator. You will answer us with that voice if we stop to ask you something.

"Also, you might flash back to where you met or last had contact with someone during that day," he continued. "At various points, your narrator may stop to ask you questions or to clarify something. Most importantly, we are looking for something called TVE. This we've found from past memory-loss cases is important to identify."

I didn't want to ask, but he must have seen the question in my face because he went on to explain, "TVE is the traumatic visual event. It is the key to unlocking your complete recall and regaining all your memory. The TVE is something that you witnessed that was so traumatic that it closed down your mind. It most likely happened around the time you received your physical injuries, your head wound, but it may be something different. You saw something, and your mind shut down to block it out."

TVE? It sounded scary to me, but Dr. Lipinski appeared used to such responses from his patients because he continued almost without a pause, "Please don't worry about the stress that recovering your memory may cause. You've been thoroughly examined, and your heart and your body are strong enough to deal with whatever we bring up. We'll be monitoring you as well, but we know going into this that your heart and your body can take it.

"So are you ready now, George? Do you have any questions?"

I nodded, indicating I was ready, and kept my mouth shut. I was officially scared shitless, but there I was—in for a penny, in for a pound.

"Okay, then," he continued. His voice was kind and gentle. "Now I would like you to turn to Mrs. Miller please and then turn to your wife and bid them farewell. Tell them that you will see them a little later when you return."

I didn't want to give away how freaked out I was, so I turned to Mrs. Miller and without missing a beat, I thanked her for all that she had done for my family and me. I told her that I'd see her when I returned. Her eyes welled up as she nodded and reached for a hankie.

Then I turned toward my wife, my loyal and loving wife.

In what I hoped was a comforting voice, I said softly, "Daddy will be right home, Irish. You'll wait for me, won't you?"

Annie kissed me gently and touched my chin. I turned back to face Dr. Lipinski and announced that I was ready. He was staring off into space, cleared his voice, and apologized.

"I'm sorry," he said. "It just hit me how important this might be."

He then picked up a remote control from his desktop and pressed a button. A large reel-to-reel tape recorder slid out of one of the panels in his office wall. He touched another button, and the wheels began to turn slowly. He spoke and began the official recording of the session.

"Firefighter George J. Bachmann will now remember and recall what he witnessed on 9/11 through the process of hypnotherapy with the help of Dr. Joseph Lipinski."

He gave some personal info and identification numbers for the case and then moved a little closer to me. I shifted in my seat; I was a bundle of nerves.

"Are you gonna swing a silver time piece in front of my eyes," I blurted out, "or do you want me to start counting backward or something?"

"No," he replied, his voice soft and calm. "I would like Mrs. Miller and Mrs. Bachmann to cover their eyes for a moment at this time."

As they did, he handed me a small monitor, like a miniature flatscreen television. On it was a swirl of colors with rainbow sprinkles, fractal geometries moving first in one direction and then another. It was strangely fascinating, and I found myself staring at it.

"That's it, George. Just keep looking at the screen." The doctor's voice sounded deeper and it echoed as if I was in a canyon and he was far, far away. I must have started a bit because he continued to assure me, "That's good, George. Don't try to fight it. Just watch the screen. And now we are going to go back to that morning in early September when … it … all … started."

I must have looked up because right behind the doctor, I saw a group of people. Some were standing up, reading the newspapers they had folded in their hands. Others were sitting down and bracing themselves as the whole room seemed to vibrate. I was confused. *What is happening?* And then I realized that I was still in Dr. Lipinski's office on the Upper West Side, but somehow I was also in a subway car, holding my firehouse laundry bag in one hand and a bag of navel oranges in the other. Then the subway train stopped, the doors opened, and I got out as if a part of me knew exactly what to do.

I made my way up the stairs and exited the Cortlandt Street station. Lower Manhattan was laid out before me, bustling in the fresh morning air. My firehouse was on the corner, and I crossed the street and headed down the block toward Liberty Street. As the South Tower came into view, I caught sight of a digital clock in a grocery store window. The time and date were easy to read from the street: "8:08 a.m. September 11, 2001."

I got to the firehouse, and our proby firefighter Shawn Tallon held the door for me. He was new, but he was a brother firefighter just like all my brothers in that house, and he was also a brother veteran, having served in the Marines. He told me that I had an outgoing detail to another firehouse that morning. I was slated to pick up my equipment and head over to Ladder 1 on Duane Street.

I dropped off the oranges in the firehouse kitchen and made my way upstairs to the third floor where my locker was. As I pulled on my uniform, the intercom shrieked, "Firefighter Bachmann, report to Ladder 10's office!" I quickly finished dressing and headed down to the second-floor office. There, I found Murray, a lieutenant with the Emergency Medical Services who was now working with the fire department's internal investigations unit. He asked me for a urine sample. It was a surprise urine test, and it came with a certain amount of paperwork. This was all part of the agreement I had signed months back as part of me getting back on the job. Because it had gotten me back on the job, I had no problem with it.

The office contained a bed, a desk, and a bathroom. The door to the bathroom was ajar, and the shower was running. Captain Paul Mallery called out from behind the steam.

"Hey, George!" he yelled. "Take care of this business before you take off on your detail at Ladder 1, will you?"

"Okay, Cap! Absolutely!" I yelled back, and then lowering my voice, I spoke to the man in front of me, "So, Murray, how's the family?"

"Fine, George," he said in his kind manner as he handed me a specimen cup and the forms I needed to fill out. "How's Annie and the baby?"

I could tell he didn't like to have to enforce these probationary things, so we were friendly about it. I sat down at the captain's desk and started on the paperwork. I thought of how, despite all these hassles, the fire department is *one big happy family.*

Suddenly a screaming rocket explosion cut through the air. The foundation of the firehouse shook with the force of it, and Captain Mallery jumped out of the shower stark naked.

"What the fuck was that?" he yelled the question in all of our minds.

I stuck my head out of the office window and looked out onto Liberty Street, but all I could see was a snowstorm of paper. What had happened and where were a mystery. But the direction of the noise and all of the office-like debris gave me a clue.

I pulled back in and yelled to my colleagues, "Something hit the tower!"

All hell had already broken out in the firehouse. We scrambled down to the apparatus floor and threw on our bunker gear. As I grabbed my helmet and jockeyed for position on the rig, I realized I was an extra man. I wasn't supposed to be here today—I wasn't scheduled to ride the Ten House rear-mount truck today. Still, this was not a normal morning. Along with my brother firefighter, Terry Rivera, I jumped on the back step of the rig and waited to take off. But there was a delay. Neither the fire truck, nor the engine seemed to be leaving the quarters. A massive throng of panicked civilians had gathered at the front of the firehouse, blocking our exit. That's what sirens are for, and finally both engine and ladder broke free of the terrified crowd, and we made our way across the street to the South Tower. (There, we were redirected to the North Tower in what would prove a lucky move. If we had committed ourselves to the South Tower elevators, none of us would have survived.)

We raced around to the North Tower, and there Rivera and I jumped off the back step. As the extra men on the rig, we had to search for extra Scott oxygen masks. Entering a building without a radio is one thing, but I didn't want to get caught without a mask in a serious situation.

Unable to locate an extra mask on our truck, I ran to another arriving engine company and commandeered a mask from them. With the mask in place, I made my way back across the street and into the lobby of the North Tower. Police officers, EMTs, and other firefighters were already there, evacuating the civilians who had arrived at their offices early that morning. I looked around for my unit. My twenty-plus years' experience told me this was the big one.

On one side of the lobby I saw a pair of human legs sticking out between a set of partially closed elevator doors. An EMT saw me and told me that there was nothing that could be done there because the plane had cut the elevator cable.

Still with that lobby in my vision, I was able to tell Dr. Lipinski that I had seen this before because this horrendous scene, with those legs, was one of the scenes in my nightmares.

Back in the trance, I continued searching through the lobby, looking for an entrance to the tower's stairwells. Reflecting off the polished marble of the lobby walls, I could see a glow, and I made my way over to investigate. In the rear of the plaza, I found a burning lake of jet fuel, an inferno spread out across Austin Tobin Plaza. I recognized this, too, from my dreams. Again, I saw what looked like two lounge chairs stuck together smack in the middle of the lake of fire. Again, I was determined to check it out. I made my way around the lake of burning fuel, shielding myself as best I could from the overwhelming radiant heat.

My breath became labored. I didn't know if it was the smoke, the heat, or my mind rejecting at that moment what my eyes saw.

"Go on, George." I heard Dr. Lipinski command and urge me. "What did you see, George? What did you see?"

The two lounge chairs were not lounge chairs. They were two airplane seats and in them were two passengers still strapped and buckled in place. It looked like they were holding hands.

"Holding hands," I heard myself murmur aloud.

Nothing could be done for them. I retreated back to the lobby.

Back in the lobby, I located a stairwell entrance and started to climb, passing an exodus of fleeing civilians. Most of them were calm.

"Was it an accident?" they asked. "Was it a small plane?"

I didn't respond. I had no more information than they did.

I continued on up, pacing myself after the first twelve flights of stairs to three or four flights at a time. The serpentine lines of exiting civilians had dwindled down to a few stragglers, and the weight of my bunker gear and mask were really starting to become evident. I finally reached what looked like a staging area on about the thirty-seventh floor. They were all on their asses; exhausted firefighters were sweating like pigs from the climb with full gear on their backs in addition to the stress of not yet knowing what the severity of the situation was.

I found two senior firefighters from Ladder 10: Mike C. and Serge. Together, we found a soda machine and used the halligan and axe to bust it open. We satiated our thirst with the sugared beverages. As we rested for a moment, catching our breaths and preparing for the next effort, the building started to rumble and shake. It went on for about eight seconds—and we were stunned into silence. Once it stopped, it seemed everyone was yelling.

"What was that?"

"What the hell …?"

I wanted to find the rest of my unit and continue up. After all, we all had jobs to do, but those of us who were ready to move were stopped dead in our tracks by Chief Picciotto. The fire chief's face was a mix of stress and authority. His voice silenced us, and we turned to him for our orders.

"A Mayday was given, men. You're all needed downstairs!" He waved his hands, backing us up. "Back down now! To the lobby level."

"But I'm trying to reach my unit, Chief!" I spoke up.

"No, no!" His voice said there was no room for discussion. "Everyone must leave the building. There are enough guys up there already."

The way he was shouting was disturbing, as if this veteran firefighter, this fire chief, was becoming undone.

Another firefighter must have noticed and started to put things together.

"What was that rumble, Chief?" he asked.

"A piece of the façade of the building fell off. That's all. That's all!" The chief's voice was steady again.

In reality, he had seen the South Tower pulverized to the ground. He realized that the death clock for the North Tower had started and gave the order only a chief could give—a Mayday. This is a historical fact conveyed in Chief Picciotto's own memoir.

He spoke like a commander when he called out, "Now, I want you men to start down. That's an order!"

As we began our descent, he yelled one more order.

"And you fuckin' guys turn around anyone you meet trying to come up. *Anyone!*"

(We started down, unaware that what we had felt—that unexplained tremor—was the South Tower crumbling to the ground, killing hundreds. We hadn't even known that the South Tower had been hit by another plane. That vital information had been kept from us by the lack of any radio communication.)

On those stairs, we were in for even more drama. Somewhere around the sixteenth floor, a small group of us ran into Captain Patty Brown and the good men of Ladder 3.

Dutifully, we passed along the message we'd been given.

"Hey, Captain Brown, a Mayday was given. They want everyone out of the building."

We relayed the message with a sense of urgency, but Captain Brown reacted no differently than if we had commented on the weather.

"Just follow me, Ladder 3!" He turned back to his men and urged them upward.

Captain Brown's crew was a rescue crew, dedicated to saving fellow firefighters. He was going upstairs to check it out no matter what, and his men were behind him. We tried to turn them around, but they refused to listen. A shoving match ensued with firefighters grabbing and pushing each other. No punches were thrown, but those of us on the descent were trying to make Brown's crew see sense.

"Cap, listen! A Mayday was given!" I grabbed Captain Brown's arm and, for a second, I thought I saw snow on the ground.

I did.

I had.

I was flashing back. I stood in front of our Brooklyn brownstone, shoveling snow. It was the winter of 1999, and I saw the captain jogging across the street.

"Hey, George," he called out to me. "You and Annie live here?"

"Indeed we do!" I called back as he crossed Union Street in his navy blue jogging suit. We stood in front of the snowy brownstone steps and talked a while.

"We heard you were floating around the Forty-Eighth Battalion, Cap," I said, as we warmly shook hands.

"Yes. That's right. What's up with you? Any luck with you and my favorite nurse having a baby?" he asked.

"It's funny you should ask, Pat," I responded soberly. "We had another procedure and we just found out this morning ..."

Patty was looking up, and I turned back to see that he was looking up at my Annie, who was standing in the open front door in her robe. She looked sick and a little disheveled, peeking out at the top of the snow-covered stairs. Patty Brown ran right to the top of those stairs and folded her in his arms, like a big brother, and she wept. I went on shoveling the snow.

All this flashed through my mind when I grabbed Captain Brown's arm on the stairs of the North Tower. I shook his mask strap to get his attention in all the confusion.

"Captain Brown," I repeated, "Chief Picciotto gave a Mayday. He wants everyone out of the building." I spoke as clearly and as quickly as I could.

"I know, George, I know."

He was brushing me off.

"Listen up, you men," he turned to address them from the top of the flight of stairs. "Ladder 3 is just going up to check it out, that's all. The rest of you guys have got your fuckin' marching orders, so take off!"

Even though he spoke with his captain's voice, none of us on the descent moved. We stood there, watching as Patty Brown and our comrades, the men of Ladder 3, disappeared up the stairs of the tower.

I continued down and realized that I'd lost Mike C. and Serge somewhere in the chaos. When I finally reached the lobby, it looked like a different world. Groups of firefighting units were huddled together, trying to figure out what to do next. A mountain of debris blocked the back entrance. The windows of the building's front that looked out over West Street seemed to be blanketed by a solid white fog. Everywhere, men were frozen in place, sensing that whatever their next move was, it might well be their last. There was no order left and no sense of a job that any of us could do. Some in the lobby took off to the right toward the pedestrian walkway bridge. I took a few steps in that direction but stopped when I felt something dripping on my shoulder. I looked: It was blood. Bodies of civilians who had jumped were hung up on the canopy overhead, and it was raining blood. People dressed as if they were out for a stroll lay on the floor in front of me and in the canopy above me. The blood turned me around and guided me toward the left, and I walked blindly into that dead white fog.

Alone, I headed out toward West Street. Something broke loose from the overhead canopy and fell right in front of me. It made an indescribable wet thump as it hit the pulverized ash at my feet. *It* was a she, a young woman in a bright floral dress. Her left arm was gone, and her left leg was barely attached. She looked like she had been in her twenties and had been pretty, but now her left eye hung from its socket and blood bubbled from the corner of her mouth. I stared for a second and made certain she was gone, no longer present in that wreck of a human body. Then I thought I heard her say something. I took my helmet off, got down on all fours, and put my ear close to her bleeding lips. She made a fist with one hand.

"Gaybe! Gaybe," she said. Her mouth was full of blood.

"What, lady? Your name is Gaybe?" I asked her.

She rolled her eyes back, swallowing the blood in her mouth and with her last breath she tried again—

I was interrupted. It was Mrs. Miller back in Dr. Lipinski's office.

"Doctor, maybe we should rest?" she asked.

The doctor would have no part of it.

"No, no. He must continue." To me, then he said, "Go on. Go on, George. What did she say? What did this poor young woman say?"

I paused, refocusing. I was back on West Street on my hands and knees with my ear beside the dying woman's mouth. She opened her clenched fist. She opened her bloody fingers, and I could see that in the palm of her hand she held an infant's toy, a small fish that was orange with white stripes.

She whispered to me as a blood bubble formed at the corner of her mouth, "Baby. My baby."

And she was still.

I left her in the toxic white fog and wandered. The haze and by my encounter with the lost mother had shattered my sense of direction. I plodded on, still uncertain of what had happened and not knowing what I could do. Then through a momentary clearing on my left, I could see that the South Tower and adjacent hotel were gone. They were simply not there, and in the foreground flames engulfed whole buildings. The white cloud drifted back, blanketing the scene again. I didn't know what I'd seen or what had happened. I was convinced at one point that a plane had hit the North Tower and dropped a nuclear device before its crash, destroying lower Manhattan. *If this is true, I am probably already poisoned,* I told myself, *and will die from the radioactivity. Just lose the mask. What is the point?* But then I thought about Annie and Tara. I had a wife. I had a child, and with them in mind, I managed to shake off the despair. I felt a new surge of will, a determination to survive—for them.

Somewhere in the middle of West Street between Liberty and Vesey, I was determined to do something—to do my job, to save others' lives as well as my own. I saw a small cluster of men emerge from the toxic, white fog. They were turning the corner, coming from the direction of the North Tower lobby. They were carrying something alabaster white, a figure, and in the dust it looked like a Michelangelo sculpture, a Pieta, with its limbs relaxed in their arms. As they passed me, I jogged to catch up.

"Can you see? Are his eyes open? Is his head up?" they shouted at me.

Another civilian victim, I thought. I concentrated on the sculpture's face in order to answer their questions. It took a few moments, and then under all that white dust, I could make out the stilled features of our beloved fire department chaplain, Father Mychal Judge. He wasn't moving *at all.*

I didn't think anything could shock me further that morning, but the day had its own agenda.

Even within my recollection when I thought upon the still face of Father Judge, I was thrown back in time to another meeting. For a flash, I was no longer on West Street surrounded by horror. I was sitting in a private room in the fire department's counseling unit, facing the department's silver-haired chaplain. In my mind, I heard his soft Irish brogue as he gently questioned me, leading me back from my own earlier precipice.

"Have you completed your twenty-eight day alcohol rehab, George?" he asked, following my so-called drug bust. It may have been a frame-up, a real piece of work, but it made me confront my real problems. I'd been drinking too much, and I knew it although I blamed it all on the stress. Father Judge had listened in his patient, quiet way as I'd told him about our fertility problems, all of the heartache Annie and I had been through, and before that the nightmares I'd carried home from Vietnam. I told him how the drinking hadn't helped. Instead, it had become a problem in its own right. And Father Judge helped me drop this one load.

"Yes, Father," I told him honestly at that point. I was proud to give him the details but humbled by the reasons for it. "I finished up at a rehab place in Pennsylvania."

"And have you completed your ninety and ninety with AA?" the chaplain asked, referring to the ninety meetings in ninety days.

"Yes, Father," I answered honestly. "I go to meetings daily in Park Slope. There are some wonderful groups there."

The silver-haired chaplain looked at me. His eyes were kind but sharp.

"I've inquired about you, son, and been told that you're on the up and up. Malachy Corrigan tells me you've even designed a unit patch for the counseling service unit."

I had made one—a firefighter busting open a bottle of booze—and Malachy, the director of the counseling service, had seen it. I thought I heard a note of praise in Father Judge's voice, but I wanted more.

"Yes, Father, I'm coming along just fine. I like serving." Serving—helping set up for the meetings and participating in the AA meetings—was part of my recovery. "But I'm a firefighter, Father, and to return to the job—"

"Hold onto your horses, son." He wanted me to slow down, I knew it. He was worried that I'd overstep, I was too vulnerable, and I'd get myself in trouble again. "There will be plenty of fires to fight. But first we pray." He closed his eyes and reached across the table to clutch my hands. Together, we bowed our heads and he asked me simply, "Do you remember your Hail Mary, George?"

"Yes, Father Judge," I replied, and then together, we began to recite the familiar words of comfort.

"Hail Mary, full of grace, the Lord is with thee ..."

In a flash, that memory was gone, and I was back, watching the men carry this lifeless body off into the dusty, white moonscape, as the echo of the prayer reverberated within me. I was more lost and disoriented than before. But around me the milky haze had started to lift. I walked a bit further and found myself in front of the North Tower. Above me, fires still blazed. I was in the middle of West Street, and I grabbed my helmet so I could look straight up the slope. The building resembled nothing so much as an enormous smoking cigar.

Dubbed the "Resurrection Patch" by Father Mychal Judge. Designed by
Firefighter George Bachmann during his short stay with Fire Department's
Counseling Service Department. It raised $300 for the NYC Burn Center.

Things were becoming clearer in my head now, too. I could
distinguish the sounds of debris falling, which was confirmed by what
I could see. But there were bodies, too; some were still on fire. I turned
and before me was a giant of a man. Although I realized it had to be an
illusion, he looked at least seven feet tall from the bottom of his boots to
the top of his white chief's helmet. It was First Deputy Commissioner
William M. Feehan. I gave a short salute and informed him that a
Mayday had been given on or about the thirty-seventh floor by Chief
Picciotto. He returned my salute.

"What do you need from me, Chief?" I asked simply,

On this day of all days, I was ready to do whatever was needed.

Just beyond Chief Feehan, I could see Chief of Department Peter
Ganci working his radio and clearly frustrated. It seemed he was having

trouble getting through. He heard my offer and turned away from his radio for a moment.

"George," he said in his deep voice, his face stern, "I need to know what's going on near the South Tower. The radios are down!"

"Right, Chief, I'll run reconnaissance in front of the tower."

"Go," he said and turned back to the malfunctioning radio.

I took off running back across West Street. *I can't believe that Chief Feehan remembered my name. I only met him once before.* (Later I told Annie how flattered I had been. After all, she had introduced us.) Unexpectedly, Dr. Lipinski's Russian accent interrupted my dream.

"You will now relive the time you first met First Deputy Commissioner Chief Feehan."

Obediently, my mind jumped back in time.

"I was going to be resworn in, after all the trouble."

Still in the trance, I felt myself traveling back to that day. I was with Annie; she was pregnant and in her last month. We'd been about to enter the revolving doors of the fire department headquarters at No. 9 Metro Tech when the rather large and distinguished-looking chief and his assistant, Chief Henry McDonald, popped out of the doors in front of us. I recognized the uniform, of course, but Annie knew them both from her own job at department headquarters.

The four of us stood facing each other, and Annie, without a moment of hesitation, spoke up.

"Chief Feehan, this is my husband, George," Annie said all fine and proper. Turning to me, she said, "Of course, you know Chief McDonald from his Ladder 114 days."

As we all shook hands, I felt awkward. *Should I apologize?* I wondered.

"Listen, Chief ..." I started to sputter like some kind of moron, caught flat-footed.

"Now, now, George," Chief Feehan stepped in with a jolly Santa Claus attitude. "Let me just welcome you back to the job and say, 'It's always darkest before the dawn!'"

I thanked both chiefs, we shook hands again, they kissed my very pregnant wife on the cheek, and all said good-bye.

In the world of Dr. Lipinski's office, Annie confirmed the meeting. My favorite witch doctor now knew that there was no threat of false memory syndrome.

Meanwhile, I drifted back to the two towers. Chief Feehan wanted a report on the South Tower. If I had to climb through hell, I was going to get whatever information I could and bring it back. I was running and running. I raced past burning bodies and burning emergency vehicles as I talked to myself to cheer myself on. *If I survive this day,* I promised myself, *I'm going to ask Annie if I can have a couple of those light beers in the basement!*

When I got to where the South Tower had stood, there was not much to see. I climbed over a piece of the building's façade. There was nothing more than a remnant of a collapsed wall and broken cement slabs jutting up from the ground and still smoldering with fire. Fires raged around me and flared up in my path, contributing to the thick smoke and obscuring my view. *This may very well be my finest hour,* I thought, *if I survive it.*

I moved on; it was still snowing ash. I made my way back to the North Tower because there was little to report of the South Tower other than its complete destruction. I stopped for a moment's breath where the tower had been split open. Electrical wiring was arcing at the bottom of the divide and spewing sparks like fireworks at Coney Island. Across this hellish canyon there were three firefighters, and they saw me. We all waved. We shared that moment, observing the arcing and sparking of what appeared to be a radiant cluster pooling below us. It was a moment of calm, like the eye of a storm.

Then I looked up at the smoking 110-story North Tower looming above us and shouted over that fiery pit, "This fuckin' smokestack won't stay up forever!"

I pointed up at the smoking tower.

"We thought we heard someone down here!" one firefighter shouted back.

"No, no! There's no time." I yelled back. I'd realized by then that they were all young and on their own. "There's no time!"

Experienced or not, they were dedicated to the job. They vanished into a dark cave that had opened up in the debris, determined to go into the tower to give whatever aid they could. As I watched them go, I saw that one had long reddish hair, like the mane on a lion. There was another one, the only one with a tool, who had an axe slung across his shoulder. The memory of my nightmares returned: the three men who I knew would most likely die were the characters from *The Wizard of Oz*. As I watched them disappear into the tower, I became increasingly aware of the invisible death clock, ticking toward the inevitable. I was already exhausted, working beyond human capacity, but I summoned whatever remained of my energy to get back to Chief Feehan and Chief Ganci at the command post in the middle of West Street in front of the North Tower. I made my report to Chief Feehan, not that I had much useful information.

The report was interrupted by the screams of a woman about fifty yards away somewhere in the white powdery fog. I was now totally exhausted. Physically drained, I sank down on one knee directly behind both chiefs, trying to catch my breath. We could all hear the screams—a woman screaming, scared, or trapped.

The haze began to lift, and suddenly we all saw her, calling for help from inside a white van that had been crushed by a South Tower girder. The back of the van was ablaze. Everything suddenly shifted into slow motion. I watched a lone firefighter grab an extinguisher from an abandoned fire engine and walk past all of us toward the van. Chief Ganci had his back to me, but Chief Feehan turned and signaled to me to assist with the rescue. I got up on my feet and followed the firefighter; carrying a water can that someone else had set down.

(He didn't know it, but Chief Feehan saved our lives—mine and the unknown firefighter's with the extinguisher—by what was to be his last order.)

As we approached the van, we saw the trapped woman, an African American, and she could see us. She was praising us and thanking us for coming to her rescue. I reached inside my turnout coat pocket, looking for a tool to break the windshield so we could get her out. She looked frightened even as she thanked God for our arrival. She was wearing a movie-themed T-shirt. It read in jagged writing and bold letters, "E.T. the Extraterrestrial."

But now everything was moving fast. That was the moment that the North Tower began to rip open. Instinctively, the lone firefighter and I tore ourselves from our efforts by the van and took cover behind a nearby girder, a remnant of the fallen South Tower. A tremor shook the earth, and I peeked over the girder, fully expecting to see the tower implode with a pulverizing black death cloud that would expand to encompass us all.

Instead, what I saw was even more startling. Chiefs Feehan and Ganci were running in our direction away from the rumbling tower. But instead of taking cover in the garage basement, a shelter behind them in 2 World Financial Center, they were running out in the open. The ten-story cloud was gaining on them, filled with the promise of death and destruction.

I must have paused because Dr. Lipinski's voice broke in.

"What happened, George?" His Russian accent rumbled through my name. "What did you see? What happened to the two chiefs?"

A shockwave, a power blast of air, blew past them ahead of the debris cloud. The force of it pushed Chief Ganci down, and his helmet came off. Chief Feehan, who was a few feet behind him, attempted to assist him. They stopped. We waved our arms and yelled at them to get their attention. We wanted them behind the girder with us where—maybe— we were safe. They couldn't see or hear us, and it was too late. Chief Ganci stood up and recovered his helmet. Both men faced each other on the ash-filled landscape of West Street. They were in the middle of a wasteland and too far from shelter. And so both chiefs, standing on the edge of infinity with no hope of survival, did what any good American soldiers do when faced with their impending deaths. They came to attention, looked to each other, and gave a full-fledged military salute. It was an acknowledgment of the other's uniform, dedication, and life. Within moments, the shockwave created by the imploding tower and the roiling dust and debris whirled past us. It was a veritable tornado, and it engulfed both men. The last thing I saw before retreating to the bottom of the girder that saved our skins was the silhouette of the two chiefs still saluting each other from inside the maelstrom.

Annie spoke aloud to Dr. Lipinski, "Doctor, I insist you wake him. He's been through enough, and he's seen more than enough!"

"There's no need to get your temper up there, Irish," I announced calmly.

Annie put her arms around me. She was crying softly.

"I don't care about the damned 9/11 Commission; I just want you to be all right for me and Tara," my Annie wept.

"Everything will be okay now, Annie," I told her. I turned to Dr.

Lipinski and said with a fair amount of certainty in my voice, "I believe we've found our TVE."

"Yes, George, the traumatic visual event was the sight of the two chiefs in their last moments. I concur, I concur!" The doctor seemed nearly to exclaim, "Eureka!" "It's all been recorded, and I shall include it in my records for medical posterity," the doctor concluded.

As my wife held me, Mrs. Miller asked quietly, "Do you know what happened after you hid under your girder, George?"

"That's a good question," I replied, eager to answer my grief counselor. "It's come back to me now, and I'd like to thank you for assisting and taking the time to come here and witness all this." I reached out to shake her hand. "Mrs. Miller, the roar of the deadly debris cloud covered the screams of the van victim, who must have perished.

I was rescued by a group of firefighters some time later, brought down to the harbor, put on a police launch on the pier, and then medevacked to a hospital in New Jersey. After that I was on the Fire Department's missing list for a few days before finally being accounted for."

We finished up the session, and I thanked everyone for his or her efforts. As we left the office, it dawned on me: With this memory, I'd recovered a new problem as well. *How the hell am I going to explain this unimaginable and unbelievable story to the 9/11 Commission?*

I shook my head as my Annie fed me two Tylenol. I would think about that tomorrow.

CHAPTER 10
Testimony Before the 9/11 Commission

After the ordeal of the session, I might have been looking for a pat on the back. But the first thing my wife said to me when we got home wasn't about courage or bravery, facing up to my fears, recalling my traumatic memories, or even my spirit on that horrible day. No, what she was on me about almost as soon as we walked in the door was my testimony to the 9/11 Commission.

"I don't think you should mention anything about any twisters," she said, "or saluting chiefs or anything like that. You don't want the fire marshals to burst into the middle of your testimony, throw a straight jacket on you, and cart you away to some loony bin somewhere, do you?"

I was silent, too traumatized to deal with her questions at that point. For a short time, I just wanted to bask in the relief and relax in the absence of the stress, headaches, and horrible haunting of not knowing, which had plagued me for so many months. Yes, I'd been skeptical, but the morning at the "witch doctor" had really helped me unload and that felt good.

But Annie did let up, so I collected my thoughts and told her that while I appreciated her candor and sensitivity, I'd have to consider how I was going to approach it. But she'd started me thinking. I had six days to prepare myself and mull over how to say what I needed to say and just how I'd present it.

I had very little idea of what to expect in terms of the commission's procedure. All I knew was the format: There were two thirty-minute sessions with a fifteen-minute break in between. An in-house grief counselor was available if I needed one at any point during or after testifying. I was supposed to show up in my Class A fire department uniform and would be sworn to tell the truth. Everything, of course, was recorded, documented, and virtually set in stone.

This was a conflict for me. I'm a simple guy, a regular guy, and I had to figure out whether under oath after swearing to tell the truth as I knew it, I was going to speak up. *Am I going to tell them all that I had witnessed, including and most particularly the last heroic moments of the two highest-ranking officers to perish on 9/11? Do they need to hear that, or is it something that only the families of those two men had the right to know?*

I had a personal debt, too. Inadvertently, the chiefs had saved my life by their final order. The least I could do was bear witness to their final moment of courage and grace and preserve it for history. The three things I searched my soul for, and knew to be true were these facts. I was the last firefighter to give Chief Feehan his final verbal report. I was the last firefighter to see Chiefs Feehan and Ganci alive. I witnessed their final salute. *But what if Annie is right? What if no one believes me?* The whole thing sounded iffy to me as well as to Annie. *Will I simply be inflicting more pain on their loved ones?*

Moreover, how would I even describe it? I was no wordsmith or intellectual. I've had little formal education unless you count a Phi

Beta Kappa in stickball, and a PhD in trading baseball cards as a kid in Brooklyn. All I had was my high school GED, what someone once called a *good enough diploma*. Oh yeah, and I had a couple of decades of fire duty experience and two Purple Hearts as a combat-experienced Vietnam veteran. But although that was a lot of life experience, it didn't make me a talker or a showman. And I didn't know if the truth that I wanted to tell was going to be a problem.

But maybe at some level, I already knew what I had to do. I had to bear witness to the bravery of the men I had respected. It was a final duty I owed those men, no matter what it might cost me. Emotionally, I was in turmoil, stressing again about what I was going to say, how I could say it, and what the repercussions could be for me, my family, and our future. Maybe Annie was right. Maybe if I spoke up, the commission would discredit *everything* I had to say and just write me off as a deranged survivor. But something deep inside me was pushing aside the doubt and encouraging—no, demanding—that I step up and relate the entirety of what I had seen.

Damn the torpedoes! My soul was ordering me, *Tell the truth and shame the devil! And isn't it the devil himself we are now at war with? And didn't the chiefs give their lives in that fight?*

I didn't know what I was risking really. I didn't know if I was putting my future in jeopardy. But come hell or high water—and I believe I'd already had a foretaste of hell—the commission was going to hear it all. The Magnificent Sighting on West Street deserved to be recorded, and the two great fire chiefs, loved and respected by a generation of New York City firefighters, deserved to be remembered as they were in their last valorous moments. Let the chips fall where they would.

The next few days passed in a blur. I must have eaten and drank. I know I slept. But all I could think about was the big day to come and all of the preparation required. Some of it was easy: I laid out my dress uniform and inspected it to ensure it was clean and well pressed. Some of it was more difficult: I'm not much of a public speaker, so I wrote an outline. Then I tore it up and wrote another. When I finally had something that kind of looked right, I tried it out. How could I just stand up and tell complete strangers what had happened to me—all of what I had done and all of what I had seen? To top it all off, I knew I had a time limit: two sessions with one break. I started timing myself with a stopwatch. What would be the point if I spent the entire time talking about the ascent up the North Tower and didn't get through it all?

Annie had an idea. What I had witnessed had already entered history by that point. She suggested that I take a look at some history books for inspiration. So, she, Tara, and I spent an afternoon looking through books at Barnes & Noble. One, on atmospheric phenomena, caught my eye. Perhaps something in there would help me explain the twister, the vortex of ash and smoke that had trapped the chiefs and, ultimately, obscured them from my view. I also reviewed several military histories, which included narratives from World War II, Korean War, and Vietnam War. There were numerous reports of how men behaved when facing capture or the grave. Survivors were quoted who had seen paratroopers and pilots bail out of their aircrafts, twist about in their chutes in their final descents, and turn toward each other to give their last salute. There was even a phrase—*turning in,* the act of twisting the parachute risers so you could face your fellow serviceman one last time. I read stories of prisoners being marched to prisoner of war camps—or worse—turning to their fellows in arms and give a final salute.

That was what I had seen on 9/11 and what I would tell the commission. First Deputy Commissioner Feehan and Chief of Department Ganci knew on September 11, 2001, that we were at war and knew as well that their part in this war was coming to an end. In a great and honorable military tradition, they accepted their fate by saluting each other in their last moments.

Before leaving the bookstore, I thought of one more book I wanted, John F. Kennedy's *Profiles in Courage*. It wasn't in stock, so I ordered it and arranged to have it delivered. I had to spend the weekend writing anyway. But every time I looked at my outline, I got up in front of the mirror, or tried my story before Annie and the baby, I doubted myself yet again. *I know what I saw. I trust my memories to be real. But do I have the nerve to tell such a fantastical-sounding tale to the commission? Do I have the guts?* This new anxiety kept me up at night, tossing and turning until the morning light outside began to creep in our bedroom window.

"Haven't you been through enough?" Annie whispered in my ear late one night. I prayed silently that my testimony would flow smoothly, and that there would be others to support what I knew to be true.

$$* \qquad * \qquad *$$

The Tuesday I was scheduled to give my testimony dawned bright and clear, just like that earlier Tuesday. *It just had to be a Tuesday,* I thought to myself.

I hadn't slept, finally gave up altogether, and got out of bed around dawn. I resorted to coffee, hoping the caffeine would wake me up and that the jitters and acid stomach would fade. After too many cups and trying to delay abandoning the comfort of our kitchen, I dressed in the Class A uniform I'd laid out days before. It was a formal dark blue uniform, complete with badges on the hat and chest, a tie, a dark blue shirt, and my spit-shined black low-quarter dress shoes. I was ready for parade duty. I slipped out of the brownstone and left Annie and Tara still sleeping.

"Hey, George!" called our mailman, who was an early bird, too. He saw my getup and started to joke with me. "Where'd ya get all those medals and ribbons?"

My Class A uniform looks rather spiffy.

"There was a sale at the fire department supply store!" I joked back.

Only when I saw his slightly startled look of surprise did I figure out the reason for his joshing: He'd thought I was on my way to yet another funeral and had been trying to cheer me up. With a weak laugh, he handed over the morning's mail—three letters and a small package. I knew if I went back inside, I might not have the nerve to head back out, so I tucked them into my black leather briefcase. Still slightly limping, I made my way to the subway to the fire department headquarters to meet with an aggressive investigative committee, the 9/11 Commission.

At 10:00 a.m. on the dot, I was there. I was ushered into a large room, something like a courtroom, and felt at once the gravity of the place. I was immediately introduced to my fire department lawyer, who remained on my left. Two fire marshals stood at parade rest behind the commission just in case anybody got excited.

Facing the three men and one woman who comprised the commission, I stood, raised my right hand, and repeated the oath. I would tell the truth, the whole truth. The American and New York state flags flanked the members of the commission, and a POW-MIA flag added a note of respect to veterans like myself. I can't say I felt better, but as I said the words, I felt resolved.

I sat at the table they had placed before the commission. The distance between us made everything more formal and frankly intimidating as if I were on trial. The microphone that was placed in fro~
my voice sound strange.

I started with the basics: my name, my rank, a
realized that I was a survivor from the firehouse c

Towers, I knew I had their attention, and I could only hope that based on my conviction and fervor, they would know that I was sober and sane. My confidence began to grow, and as it did, I gave them, as I had sworn, the whole truth.

I started with the events of that morning. I told them I had just reported for work when we heard what we thought was an explosion and that we had all rushed over to the scene. I related the events leading up to Chief Picciotto's Mayday, which we'd received on what I thought was the thirty-seventh floor of the North Tower. I recounted our run-in with Captain Patty Brown and the men of Ladder 3, and our brotherly skirmish on the sixteenth floor. I told them about the first victim I had seen, the woman who had jumped from the tower, who was clutching a small child's toy in her fist.

From then on, it was like my dream, only I knew what was coming. I told them about the toxic white fog and about seeing fellow firefighters carrying the still body of Father Mychal Judge. I described reaching the command post, and how it was blazing away on the edge of imminent collapse. I told them Chief Feehan ordered me to recon at the South Tower because the radios were all down and so I was sent to give an eyewitness report on what was happening on the other side.

That brought us up to our scheduled break time, fifteen minutes to catch my breath. I went out into the hallway and tried to think of what I would say when we went back in. I couldn't call Annie because no outside phone calls were allowed. But I had to figure this out for myself anyway. My head was pounding. *Why me?* I thought. *How did I get here?*

I started searching through my bag. I knew I had Tylenol, and I believed Annie had stashed an energy bar in there, too. Rooting around, I came across the morning's mail. Just for a distraction, I opened the package. It was the copy of *Profiles in Courage* that I'd ordered only days before.

Could anything be clearer? I swallowed down two Tylenols for the headache, but my uncertainty had dissipated on its own. When the attendant called me back into that room, I hardly needed the reminder that I was still under oath and obligated to tell the whole truth.

And I didn't hold back. I told them everything I had seen—how the enormous pressure of the collapse of the North Tower had formed a seismic shockwave of air that had knocked Chief Ganci down; how Chief Ganci had recovered and replaced the helmet that had fallen from his head; how, in that last moment as both chiefs had realized the hopelessness of their situation, they had turned to each other, saluted, were then engulfed by the vortex, and were gone.

I was glad I had done the bookstore research. As I retold the events of that day, I had added some scientific detail. I explained to the commission how the pancake-like collapse of the tower could have created a twister. I explained that the force of the displaced air from the collapse must have swept along the narrow length of West Street until it had met the alley, creating a toxic twister that shot out and spun toward the two chiefs. The force the winds had created had kept the debris at bay momentarily, clearing the air for that one final salute. It was an odd moment, sure, but scientifically possible—the physics behind the catastrophe had permitted me to watch as two beloved fire department officers had accepted their fate together and acknowledged their mutual respect before they were overwhelmed and then gone.

I couldn't tell how my testimony was received. All I knew was that I was telling the truth. But once done, I started to see signs that they hadn't believed me. They were passing notes to each other and leaning over to whisper in each other's ears. Maybe it was my imagination, but it seemed like every time I opened my mouth after a certain point, the female commissioner rolled her eyes.

One of the men asked me about that final salute, almost as though he wanted to but could not believe me. I was prepared. I told them about the World War II pilots I'd read about and how turning in had a history in the military. But I had the feeling they thought I was shining them on, making up a story to glorify the two men I had so deeply respected.

I started to get a little peeved.

"Listen," I told them, leaning forward on the table. "I'm sure the good people of this panel have heard a lot of different stories. But I'm not some fireman who got dusted by debris a couple of blocks away from the epicenter. I was there right by the North Tower. I was rescued from within the epicenter on West Street, Quadrant 1. I was less than thirty feet away from where two of our highest-ranking officers were killed in the worst attack on U.S. soil since Pearl Harbor. Just check your virtual maps.

"Liquid, pulverized ash flowed there," I was on a roll. "Superheated gasses seared the air, and tremors tossed full-sized fire trucks up in the air like toys. This was not your ordinary building collapse, and the atmosphere—the very air around us—acted in strange ways. That's why what I saw matters. These were two chiefs delivering a slap to the face of certain death, standing up with courage and honor in the middle of a manmade hell, in the middle of a battlefield—the first on the U.S. mainland since the end of the Civil War. Their actions echoed their forefathers, the brave men who served in Valley Forge, at the Alamo, on the Bataan Death March, and, yes, at Pearl Harbor. May I be damned to eternal hell if I'm not telling what I believe to be the truth about these honorable men."

I paused and then thanked the commission for their time. Everyone, each commissioner included, was near tears, and I stumbled a little reaching for my bag. Even if they hadn't believed me, at least they were moved by my fervor.

As I waited for the elevator, I was conscious of my breathing, trying to quell the shaking in my limbs. *I did it. I faced that fear and told the entire story.* I couldn't wait to tell Annie and Tara. But even as I waited for that elevator, a small group of men; two men in uniform, fire chiefs, and a civilian in a suit with a crabbed little face; came up behind me. The elevator arrived, and I got in. Although the suit didn't, he reached over to hold the door open. I could see something nasty in his faint smile.

"I know all about you," he said like some cartoon villain. "I hear you play guitar at the firehouse, and now you're setting yourself up as some kind of Jimi Hendrix of 9/11."

His tone was sly, insinuating, and mean.

"The story of the two chiefs is true, Commissioner Scoppetta."

Yes, I'd recognized his cartoonish face. It was the new fire commissioner, Nicholas Scoppetta. He wasn't a fireman, just a politician who had come in with the Bloomberg administration. He was often described by other firefighters as looking like Mr. Magoo from the 1960s television show.

He smirked at me and sneered, "And who will you be telling this tall tale to, George?"

He even sounded like Jim Bacchus.

"Only every good American, sir."

I'd already done the hard part. I knew I was in the right.

"And how do you propose to get that *story* out?"

I didn't like his tone, his insinuations, or his smug grin. I took his hand off the elevator door so it could close. I wanted to go home. (Later I found out what a standup guy he really is.)

"Just move over, Rover," I said to that smiling face, "and let Jimi take over."

I couldn't be sure, but as the door closed, I thought I saw the two chiefs behind him smiling.

*　　*　　*

"So, how'd it go?" Annie met me at the door, her face a mixture of concern and relief. I was smiling and clearly okay. "Tell me, George!"

"Well, I think they may ask for my uniform and citations back real soon," I replied. I dropped my briefcase on the floor and reached over to take my wife in my arms. "And I wouldn't be counting on that pension."

Annie pushed me back and away.

"Nice. Nice going." She looked up at my face in disbelief. "Way to go, bucko," she said and turned away.

Chapter 11
Receiving the Double Star

It had been several days since the hearing, and Annie was still not talking to me. How could I blame her? I'd gone against her advice and common sense really and testified under oath to the 9/11 Commission about what must have sounded like a fairy tale.

Although the scientific data I had reviewed supported my recollections, it must have sounded like nutty talk. I'd told the truth, the gut-wrenching, soul-stirring truth, but I couldn't help feeling like their collective reaction was that of pity.

"There's some psychosis in the house," I thought I had heard one of the panel members say.

Then to top it all off, I had that confrontation with Scoppetta. I had actually talked back to him! I'd told him that whether or not he believed it, I was going to tell anyone who cared what I had seen. In essence, I'd told him that whatever he, the NYC Fire Commissioner thought, didn't matter. I was sticking with my story.

No wonder I was in the doghouse. Forget about all of the years she and I had spent serving the same department, I knew Annie was worried about our future. We had a daughter, and she had a daddy who was in no condition to go back to work even if he were allowed to.

But what else could I have done? First Deputy Commissioner William Feehan and Chief of Department Peter Ganci were more than longtime veteran firefighters; they were two of the most respected men in the department—maybe in the whole city. Since the 1970s whenever a major fire made it onto the news and someone had to assure the public, there was Chief Feehan or Chief Ganci addressing the press. Look back at any photo of the St. Patrick's Day parade, and there they were. Up in front and usually right beside the mayor, the photos in the fire department archives depict Chief Feehan leading the department and Chief Ganci walking with Mayor Giuliani. Perhaps most importantly, they were family men, both of them, and both had sons on the job. These men were firefighters' firefighters, heart and soul.

But maybe family was the issue. *How do you think the families will take to this fantastic tale?* a little disconcerting voice in my head nagged at me. *Will it sound crazy to them? Will it sound like you're bragging about your time with their loved ones?* I tried to shake it off, but it was hard. *Have I done something wrong?*

Of course, this led to another potential hotspot: survivor guilt. Had I been wrong to testify to what I did was just one question. *Had I done wrong in surviving when other men—possibly greater men—had not?* Logically, I knew it was the luck of the draw. There will always be good men who are killed in any attack, but that knowledge didn't help when I looked around and saw that I was healing, could breathe and see, and still had a life to live. They couldn't and didn't. *Do I have any right to be here alive and testifying to it all?*

That malignant voice continued to nag at me. I had only one answer, *Tell the truth and shame the devil.* The truth was my only defense, my only recourse. The truth was the closest I could be to God. I was sober;

I believed I was sane. I had felt an obligation and a duty to bear witness to a brave final act. So be it.

I was no spinner of tales. If anything, I was the reticent type, shy. It took the guys in my old firehouse years to find out that I was a Vietnam vet and that I'd seen combat and been injured. I had seen my share of the world's horrors, but I usually preferred to keep those things to myself—except this time. This time, speaking out seemed to be the only honorable thing to do.

Still, I couldn't blame Annie for her silent treatment. As far as we knew, I'd risked everything: my disability, our 9/11 compensation, and our future. Her silence fit my mood, and I plodded around the big, old house depressed. Only when I was praying with Tara did I feel relief. I asked God if I had done the right thing and tried to trust in the inner voice that told me I had. I spoke to the two chiefs, too, during those long nights. In my mind, they were like consoling fathers, gentler and more understanding than my stepdad had been, and just as they had guided me on the job, so they listened to my prayers.

*   *   *

It was about a month later, and I heard Annie squeal excitedly. She was talking to me again by then, and I don't think I'd heard happiness in her voice since I had testified. Still, I recognized the sound right away—from the Annie I remembered and love.

"George, George, it's for you!" She was calling me from the kitchen. "It's Captain Engel!"

She was nearly hopping up and down with excitement by the time I got downstairs. I was somewhat more mobile by then, but it still took me awhile to get around. Captain Engel was the new captain of Ladder 10.

"George," he said to me once I had picked up, "we need you to come down to the new Ten House on Liberty Street on Thursday. You and a couple of the other survivors are going to get a citation—the mother of all citations—from the commissioner."

"Are you sure, Cap?" I couldn't quite get my mind around the idea that Commissioner Nicholas Scoppetta was going to give me an award. *The sour-faced little guy must have believed me after all!* "You sure?"

"Yes, yes!" The captain was fairly yelling into the phone. "He wants you to come down and get your citation. He says you're gonna need it!"

His words went right through me.

"Hallelujah," I sighed, as much as said.

Validation. Perhaps this was the light after the darkness that Chief Feehan had foretold.

And so that Thursday, I again donned my Class A uniform and returned to my old stomping grounds. The rebuilt, renovated version of my old firehouse was ablaze in sunlight, nestled on the very edge of Ground Zero. The new Ten House was being launched in style. Everyone was dressed sharp in Class A uniforms. Flags were waving, and everyone's family and kids were on the scene. The fire trucks were parked outside, and there were so many tourists and visitors that the police department had cordoned off the area.

But as we waited for the politicians and dignitaries to arrive with their speeches in hand, we began to notice how few of us there really were—how many of us were missing. The loss became more obvious as we were called to formation. There were so few of us that we formed a single line.

Captain Engel addressed the crowd with a few introductory words of thanks and pride and then read the list of names—the short list of names—from the paper before him. Annie and Tara were bursting with excitement, clapping and cheering when I was called up. I marched to the podium where the captain of the firehouse waited and stood tall, chest out, as he presented me to the crowd.

"Firefighter First Grade George J. Bachmann by order of the Commissioner of the Fire Department you are hereby a recipient of the New York City Fire Department's highest-rated citation: the World Trade Center Rescue Recovery Double Star Memorial Citation. We thank you."

He pinned the medal and a ribbon on my chest. The ribbon had two gold stars set against purple and black and the number 343, the number of firefighters we lost that day, engraved in gold lettering. (To this day, I wear that medal and ribbon at all parades and other formal functions, opposite my heart.) Later we learned that I was the only combat Vietnam veteran to ever win this prestigious New York City Fire Department highest-rated citation. The citation was considered by some to be the medal of honor of 9/11.

We traded salutes, and I marched off, trying to hide my little limp, back to the formation of lucky, proud, and heroic survivors. Annie's tears flowed, revealing her pride and relief as she held Tara up to see her daddy, standing tall that day. We took pictures and shook hands with the others. I told everyone I would see them on the anniversary in September, but the absence of everyone who wasn't there burdened the glory of that golden day: my wonderful friends and brother firefighters, Ladder 105 and the heroic Captain Vinny Brunton, Lieutenant Mike Quilty, Lieutenant Glen Perry, Lieutenant Phil Petti, and all the members of Squad One, and firefighter Vinny Kane of Engine 22, a personal friend who Annie and I both considered a member of our family.

I thought of these lost heroes, men I had known and loved, along with the men of my own Ten House. I made a vow then and swore to them and to myself that I would try to live a good, clean life for my little family the rest of my time on this earth. That day seemed like a good start. The tears we, because I was not alone in these thoughts, felt welling up behind our eyelids did honor to those who were gone. There was nothing to be ashamed of here and much to be proud of.

By late afternoon we were back home—exhausted but happy. My leg ached, and I sat down to rest it while Annie carried Tara, already half asleep, to bed. When Annie came back down to join me, she looked more relaxed than she had in ages. Even my Annie, who had been so worried, had to admit that maybe the worst was over.

"Just maybe," she acknowledged to me as she took the other easy chair in our living room, "just maybe everything will be all right after all."

What we didn't know could still hurt us though. We were relaxing and letting our guard down now, but we had one fight left ahead of us. We were in for one hell of a finale.

CHAPTER 12

The Overdose Death Dream

I hadn't had a drink in the many months before 9/11. And since then, I really couldn't afford to slip up. I had a young child at home, and my wife was showing signs of postpartum depression, not to mention that she was still taking care of me and serving as my own personal nurse as I continued my slow recovery from a barrage of injuries—physical, mental, and spiritual. I had been readmitted to the hospital for my injuries on one occasion since 9/11, a visit that lasted for about a week before I was released again. The gnawing pains from my back and crushed skull were still there, only slightly tempered by the regular epidural shots that numbed me from the spine out. Still, I counted my blessings. I tried to enjoy everything I still had—that I could simply be and that I was alive and with my Annie and our little sweet pea, Tara.

But it was still tough. All of the reasons and stress that had started my drinking years before were still there. We hadn't heard anything about my disability. Instead, we were stuck waiting out the bureaucratic logjam between the 9/11 board and the New York Fire Department for word on my status. It was nerve-wracking, to say the least. Between the pain and the stress, I wanted to drink. But I had Tara to think about, and Annie had taken care of me enough. It was my turn to care for her. And so I tried to arm myself. I fortified myself with vitamins and tried to strengthen and stretch my aching muscles with exercise. I tried to ease the emotional stress as well and went forward with my therapy, digging into some of the inner conflicts that I had carried with me for years. Although it may have clarified them for me—yes, my parents had neither been warm nor supportive; yes, I wanted something better for my daughter—it didn't make them go away. Moreover, something was welling up inside me, something dark. I could feel it. I didn't know what to expect. I just knew something was coming.

As a nurse, Annie was already privy to one of the dark secrets of 9/11 survivors. As a result of her work at the department's headquarters, she knew the numbers and had heard the rumors. She knew that 9/11 was still claiming its victims. Incidents of overdoses and suicide attempts were surfacing. Survivor's guilt was hounding far too many people into their graves. What we didn't know then was how close I would be to becoming such a statistic.

The day seemed so promising. Annie was taking Tara on an excursion. They were going over to New Jersey to visit her brother Joe. His wife and kids adored Tara, and the family had a beautiful house. She deserved a visit with her family—and a break from me, to be honest. Besides, it was good for Tara to get to know her cousins and give them a chance to spoil her a little. We all kissed good-bye, and I promised that I'd stay indoors because when the temperature dropped, all my injuries acted up. It was the first time I'd been home alone since being released from my rehospitalization, Annie reminded me that I should be careful.

In response, I showed her the list of the projects I'd made for myself. I was going to disinfect the bathroom, bring down the laundry, and put the dishes in the dishwasher. I figured I could use the time to be handy around the house and get some work done. In truth though I was also thinking about the Yankees game—and a cache of beers I had hidden in the basement. It seemed innocent enough and a reward for all of the chores I intended to do. *What's baseball without a beer? It was broad daylight, after all, and this was America's pastime.*

I waved good-bye from the top of the stoop, and little Tara waved back as her mom helped her down the street. Then by habit I locked up and activated the security system. I headed downstairs and retrieved one of the six packs, chilled and ready for consumption. While I was down in the basement, I also picked up one of my old fire department scrapbooks and, with the beer, carried it upstairs to our living room. I sat down with the scrapbook in front of me and pulled the tab on a can of beer. It opened with a soft click, the sound of a thousand innocent beverages, and I took a sip. I didn't realize then what I had unleashed with that click.

(In retrospect, I should have been more aware. I'd spent enough time at AA by then to know that when an alcoholic picks up a drink after a long dry spell, he is asking for trouble. The reactions vary. Some people in recovery report having had hallucinations as a result of the way their body chemistry reacts to the alcohol. I didn't yet know or consider what it would do to me.)

I was looking at a picture in my scrapbook of Chief Joseph Grzelak of the Forty-Eighth Battalion. He was one of the veterans who hadn't made it through 9/11. We had a lot in common, including active military service; he used to be a door gunner for the leathernecks in Vietnam. We'd posed for that photo together out in front of my old Brooklyn firehouse with Sparky, the firehouse's nasty Dalmatian, and a bunch of neighborhood kids. We had our hands on each other's backs, and despite that dog's tendency to snap, we all looked happy—together. I guess that set me off a little bit—a good man and those good times gone.

Enough of this, I had the sense to tell myself. Time to watch the game. But when I switched the television on, something else caught my eye. It was a 9/11 documentary, and Mayor Giuliani was being interviewed.

The interview, I realized, was an old one, done a week after that horrible day. In it, the mayor was recounting the last time he had seen his "two favorite fire chiefs," as he referred to them, on that fatal morning. He was talking about Chiefs Feehan and Ganci, of course.

"I was on West Street; the South Tower had already collapsed," said the mayor with the pain of that day etched on his face. "I was watching in horror as people began to leap to their deaths from the North Tower. I saw something I'll never forget: A man and a woman held hands and then jumped together.

"I was shaken to my soul, and I turned and asked Chief Ganci, 'Can we save any of these people?'

"Chief Ganci replied, 'Your Honor, we can save only those from the fire line on down.'"

The mayor continued, "First Deputy Commissioner Chief Feehan was with us, too. We discussed the necessity of setting up a command post closer to the site to coordinate rescue efforts. The last time I saw them that day they were both running in the direction of tower one, the North Tower, to set up the post. We didn't know it—well I certainly didn't—that the collapse of the structure was imminent."

Mayor Giuliani was silent and he looked down. Then–Police Commissioner Bernie Kerik and Fire Commissioner Thomas Van Essen both reached over and gave him a pat on his back, a small touch of consolation.

The mayor looked up and said simply, "We're going to miss them."

That was enough. I turned the television off and started to drink in earnest. I needed to dull the pain. That's the worst kind of drinking, of course. Alcohol is a depressant—it makes everything worse and nothing better. But I wanted to be numb. I wanted to stop feeling what I felt, but a crazy desire seized my mind. I wanted to thank the chiefs for saving my life. I was going to thank them and go see them in my dream state where I could greet them properly and thank them for what they'd done. So clutching the two remaining cans, I staggered up the stairs to our bedroom.

It wasn't a death wish—not consciously. Somewhere in my stupor, I thought I'd simply be able to reconnect with them, communicate, and then sleep it off. *I'll be back before Annie and Tara get home,* I thought. But at another level, the guilt was dragging me down. *Why had I survived when such good men had not? It should have been me. I should have ...*

Despite the clumsy fingers of drunkenness, I managed to change into my full dress uniform. It seemed important to look my best if I was going to see my chiefs. I checked myself out in the full-length mirror we kept in the bedroom. I looked like a man of honor. I stood up straight, puffing out my chest to play up my double-star citation, the ribbon, and the medal. I checked out the Ten House patch on my left arm. Then I put on my cap with its badge and chugged another beer. *I'll be back before they get home,* I thought. *I'll even have time for a shower.*

The booze was already doing its part. I stumbled and nearly fell as I made my way into the bathroom. Was I thinking clearly? No, but that's alcoholism for you. Alcohol and survivor guilt are a potentially lethal combination, but I was denying the obvious as I rifled through the medicine cabinet. *I just want to see them again,* I told myself oblivious to the consequences. *I just want one more chance to speak to them, to salute them, and to tell* them *what I witnessed.*

I took the bottle of blue sleeping pills back into the bedroom. Then I reached into my wallet for the funeral cards—their mass cards. Propping them up on the nightstand, I sat on the bed and looked into their faces. I thought to myself that I had had things pretty good. There were no major complaints. *But in my next life, I hope that I'd have someone like those two old-timers for a father. Next time, next life …*

It was as close as I came to acknowledging what I was doing. But before I could follow that train of thought, I wrenched off the cap, jiggled out a pill, and downed it quickly with a swig of beer.

"Don't try this at home, folks," I said to nobody in particular.

I was mustering my courage. I lay down on the bed and held the pill bottle up in front of me. Through the clear plastic, I could see the remaining pills.

"To sleep, perchance to dream."

Was that Shakespeare? Those lines went through my head as I focused in. *The dream was the thing, right?* I'd tried to tell the commission that day. I had told them the truth of what I had seen—of the bravery of those men. But all they had heard was a dream, and they had dismissed it.

"I've—become—an emissary—of death."

The words rattled around in my buzzing brain, forcing me up. This wasn't peace. This wasn't dreaming. I upended the bottle, swallowed several of the pills, and lay back down again with my hands neatly folded at my sides as if I were standing at attention instead of lying prone on our big bed.

I was feeling fine. I was making good speed, too, and for the first time in ages, my back didn't hurt. Yes, I knew at some level that I was still in my bed and that I'd numbed myself to the point where I probably couldn't tell if my back was aching at all, but the drugs had started to kick into my mind—and with them, the dreams. I was moving along and feeling very spiffy in my dress uniform with my badges and my ribbon. Very, very spiffy.

I was in a long and straight corridor now where my spit-shined dress shoes clicked neatly on the highly buffed floor. Smart and sharp, I strode toward a big double glass door. Through it, I could see orange, all orange. There was a man in a dark suit with a crew cut standing in front of the doors. His hands were folded in front of him. He looked like he could be packing heat, and his posture was no nonsense. As I approached, he looked me up and down, catching sight of my unit patch.

"You want in here, Ten House?"

"Yes, I do, Fire Marshall Garcia," I answered. I wanted him to know that I knew that *he* was New York City Chief Fire Marshall Louis F. Garcia.

"What do you have in your pockets?" His tone was all business with a slight Latino accent.

I pulled out my white parade gloves with my left hand and with my right, to my surprise, a little red flashlight—the kind you'd find on a firefighter's helmet.

"What the fuck? You 'specting a fuckin' blackout or something?" His accent became more noticeable as he seemed to relax.

"No, Fire Marshall Garcia. But can you tell me where I am?"

I was trying to be polite because I didn't want to waste time being provoked by him.

"You're at 2 World Financial Center," he told me. "Down that hall is the exit to West Street across from where the North Tower was."

"And inside?" I inquired, pointing through the glass doors—to the orange beyond.

"This is the Circle of Heroes Foundation," he said. "They're about to reveal something of historical significance, but no one knows what it

125

is." He stood up straight, effectively barring the door. "No one comes in without an invitation. But …" He paused, looked around. "Considering you're from the firehouse up the block and your uniform is in order, I'll let you in. Just do me a favor there, Ten House. Keep the flashlight in your pocket."

"Yes, sir."

I saluted as he reached for one of the doors and held it open so I could enter. I strolled in. I found myself at the back of a large auditorium. The entire room had an orange tinge to it. I noticed that the sound was good; it had been built with acoustic integrity. The sound was so clear in fact that it was actually in your face even way back where I stood.

There was no one in any of the seats. Instead, everyone was crowded before a long table in front of the raised stage area. On the stage was a tall wooden podium with a golden microphone on top. The podium was decorated with a huge emblem, a larger version of the shoulder patch worn by all New York City Fire Department personnel. At the back of the stage was a huge white projection screen flanked by tall, dark green curtains that ran to the edge of the stage.

I made my way down the aisle and toward the stage. As I got closer, I recognized some of the faces in the crowd. There were a few politicians and other local celebrities. I saw the District 1 Councilman Allen J. Gerson, talking to *New York Daily News* columnist Michael Daly. There was my old division chief, Peter Hayden, famous among some of us for calling Mayor Bloomberg's administration "empty promises by empty suits." He was chatting with Dennis Smith, author of many fire department related books, including *Report from Ground Zero*. There was Scott Stringer, the Manhattan Borough president, conversing with Fox 5 reporter and ex-detective Mike Sheehan. A cornucopia of high-ranking civil servants mingled among the notables. A banner over the projection screen read, "Circle of Heroes." There was a stir at the back of the auditorium and a circle of men, clearly bodyguards, briskly entered through the glass doors. At the center of the group was Donald Trump, the real estate magnate. Only the week before, he'd been on television, encouraging New York to rebuild the Twin Towers as they once were. A tap on the shoulder startled me. I turned around and found my childhood buddy, Dennis Hamill, now a renowned columnist and author, standing there.

"Now I know I'm dreaming!" I sputtered.

We hugged like brothers and then shook hands to top it off.

"Hey," I asked him, "when are you gonna pay up for all those Spaldeens you and that old crew of yours used to hit over the roofs on Thirteenth Street?"

He laughed a little at my childhood reminiscence.

"How's our favorite nurse and your lovely daughter doing?"

"Fine, Dennis, fine."

We could have kept on talking, but it had become obvious that something was happening onstage.

"Good to see you, Georgie. Looks like they're starting now. I'll have to talk to you later," said Dennis, waving so long and in the same motion reaching for his reporter's notebook and a pen from his jacket pocket. Now appearing onstage behind the podium was the man I had traded words with after my testimony before the commission, Fire Commissioner Nicholas Scoppetta. He adjusted the microphone, and I tried to keep in mind that despite his unkind words, it was because of his stamp of approval that I had received the department's highest-rated citation.

Tonight, though, his voice wasn't harsh or mocking. Instead, it was kind and soft like a long-lost uncle. He spoke into the microphone, and after some feedback, he moved away from it a few inches.

"Hello. Can you hear me?"

Someone in the crowd nodded, and there was a murmur of assent.

"Okay, then, we'll start." He paused. "I am Fire Commissioner Nick Scoppetta for those who don't know me. And I'd like to welcome everyone to this closed meeting and brief invitation-only presentation of the Circle of Heroes Foundation.

"The Circle of Heroes events are usually held at No. 9 Metro Tech, the department's Brooklyn headquarters, when it pertains to the fire department. But 2 World Financial Center requested that we have this somewhat historical event right here, and because they hold all the cards now, we're here.

"Before I introduce some of our guests, I'd first like to explain what the purpose of this little get-together is." He paused, looked up, and pointed toward the back of the room. "Outside these doors," he said, "during the attacks on the World Trade Center, something took place that is just now coming to light. Something we now refer to as 'The Magnificent Sighting on West Street.'"

I couldn't have been more surprised. *This man had doubted me!* But even as I heard my own sharp intake of breath, he continued.

"To understand The Magnificent Sighting on West Street, one must consider two central factors. First, the atmospheric conditions ..."

He went on to briefly summarize the atmospheric anomalies created by the collapse of the North Tower and the ensuing shockwaves— exactly the same conditions I had researched and to which I testified.

"Second," he said, "we must consider the last heroic moments of the two highest-ranking fire department officers to perish on 9/11. At first, the sighting was thought to be a rumor—a wish fulfillment, if you will. But today, I can assure you, ladies and gentleman, we will lay this rumor to rest!"

He paused and looked around. Everyone was spellbound.

"We will discuss this subject in greater depth later. But now, we would like to thank the authorities of 2 World Financial Center for their accommodations and evidence that they have contributed to our understanding of this historic event." Scoppetta stopped again, but just for a second. "I'd like at this time to thank the heads of the New York City Police, Port Authority, and Fire Marshals for sending representatives. I'd like to thank the media for sending their small contingent of reporters, as well as the honored politicians, dignitaries, and special guests floating around. One more thing, we ask that you hold your questions and picture taking 'til the end of this event."

The commissioner then asked to general surprise that we join together for a short prayer. Without waiting for a response, he stepped back from the podium and bowed his head. For a few moments, nobody knew what to think. Suddenly a familiar voice boomed out from the speakers distributed throughout the auditorium. It sounded as though it was coming from heaven. It also sounded familiar.

"This is Father Mychal Judge, chaplain of the New York City Fire Department. Please join me in a prerecorded version of the Lord's Prayer. 'Our Father, who art in Heaven, hallowed be thy name ...'"

As the deceased chaplain's rich Irish brogue rang out, everyone in the crowd removed their hats and bowed their heads.

"... and deliver us from evil. Amen. In the name of the Father, and of the Son, and the Holy Spirit. Amen."

It *was* Father Judge. The prerecorded prayer was a surprise and a sad reminder of his loss. As we lifted our heads, it seemed we all shared a sense of the importance of this gathering.

In a softer voice, reflecting the new solemnity of the occasion, Commissioner Scoppetta thanked us.

"To lead the remainder of this meeting, I would like to introduce New York City Fire Department Chief of Operations Salvador Cassano," he said.

With that, a Clark Gable look-alike, down to the pencil-thin mustache, stepped up to the podium to a small round of applause. Commissioner Scoppetta patted him on the back and walked off, leaving Chief Cassano to fend for himself.

Chief Cassano adjusted the microphone and began to speak, clearly comfortable in front of an audience, "Thank you, Commissioner Scoppetta, and thank you, ladies and gentlemen. I'm not one for mincing words, so let's get right down to business."

A slightly puzzled buzz went through the crowd.

Cassano kept talking. "As the commissioner said, our goal is to bring the so-called rumor of the Magnificent Sighting on West Street to a final conclusion. Tonight, we're going to lay it to rest.

"Because of the sensitivity of the subject matter, we'll address this matter in a straightforward and truthful manner with all respect to the families." He turned a page of what must have been his prepared statement. "There are different ways to explain this sighting.

"However, this is how I choose to describe it. On September 11, 2001, when the South Tower collapsed, killing hundreds of Americans, including many rescue workers, it fell in an uneven pattern. Multiple floors fell together in varying directions. Ten floors in one direction, fifteen floors in another, and this process continued until little other than a few stories near the base remained. However, the North Tower fell in what we refer to as a 'perfect pancake collapse.' Most of you know that, it is after all well-documented fact, but you may not know exactly what that means.

"Imagine, if you will, a child's long balloon pointed upward and standing tall like that tower. Then imagine slowly releasing the air from the opening at its bottom. If you can imagine this balloon being a 110-story megastructure with the air surging out from its base, then you can see how such a collapse created a seismic shockwave of air, which rushed out—arriving moments ahead of the falling pulverized debris."

Heads in the crowd nodded. That made sense.

"We submit that this shockwave of air hit the walls of this building outside on West Street and bounced back," he continued. "Generating a vortex in the alley behind the octagonal building on the corner. Because this intensely pressured air had no place to go, it spun out to the middle of the street." He paused and looked out at the crowd. "By now, you may be asking yourselves, what does this have to do with the price of beans?"

A few nervous laughs were heard from the audience.

"But you must understand the physics of the collapse in order to comprehend what happened."

The chuckling gave way to nods. We were with him.

Chief Cassano signaled to a projectionist, and the auditorium went dark. Then he gestured to the screen behind him. Before him in the audience, some of the city's most notable, most powerful men waited, like excited children, to see what would happen next. An image appeared on the screen.

"This is a photo taken by a weather satellite from space above the site at the exact moment of impact of the North Tower." He turned on a red laser pointer and led our eyes to a particular pattern in the image on the screen. "Please note these swirly bowties, these blurry round images here." The red laser light made small circles on some circular clouds. They looked like coils, twisting the air. "One small twister is seen coming out near Austin Tobin Plaza and this other larger twister here on the satellite image is hovering in the middle of West Street." With his red pointer, Chief Cassano circled the swirling cloud on the screen. "It's this tornado, which existed for only a brief time on West Street, that is our point of interest. Remember it. We'll return to the atmospheric phenomena later, but now we would like to talk about the command post set up in front of the North Tower."

He seemed happy to be changing the subject. After a brief pause, he continued, but his tone was different—prouder.

"First Deputy Commissioner William M. Feehan and Chief of Department Peter Ganci," he announced as suddenly their pictures, both smiling side by side, appeared on screen. Photos, pictures of both men with their children and grandchildren marching in the Columbus Day and St. Patrick's Day parades, flashed by as Chief Cassano recited their histories. His voice was full of affection and respect. "The highest-ranking officers set up and manned the command post in front of the blazing North Tower although its collapse was imminent." There was pride and sadness in his voice as he said, "This brings us to the statements given to the 9/11 Commission surrounding the last moments of these beloved chiefs. Testimonials, given to the 9/11 Commission by surviving firefighters and officers and by survivors who were rescued beneath the rubble on West Street, indicate that in the moments before they perished, the two chiefs turned to each other and gave each other a final salute."

FIRST DEPUTY FIRE COMMISSIONER

WILLIAM M. FEEHAN

A deep murmur rose from the audience. Chief Cassano put his hand up to signal us to quiet down, and the lights came up slightly, illuminating the high profile crowd.

"We really had no way of proving if this ever really happened," he continued, "so we compiled all of the anecdotal information we had together with eyewitness testimony and came up with a matrix of computer-generated animation just to see what it might have looked like."

Chief Cassano gave another signal. The auditorium lights dimmed again and an animated sequence appeared on the screen. On a matrix grid, the animated figures of both chiefs stood side by side in their white helmets. Using his laser, Chief Cassano pointed out the chiefs. A timer to the left of the image showed the seconds passing by.

"At exactly 10:28:31," he continued, "the North Tower began its perfect pancake collapse. The two chiefs were seen running down West Street. Chief Ganci fell, most likely due to a back blow from the seismic shockwave that passed them and knocked off his helmet. Both men recovered, came to attention, and then saluted each other just as a large vortex engulfed them."

Almost immediately after he had finished these words, the lights came on in the auditorium to reveal a crowd pale and stricken with expressions of the oh-so-familiar 9/11 grief. Surprisingly, no one had left early in distress.

Chief Cassano gave the crowd a couple of seconds to recuperate and then started up again, "We had no way of proving that this ever happened." He sounded angry. His words separated with emotion. "We had no—real—proof. Until now!"

As one, the crowd leaned forward, and Chief Cassano leaned toward us.

"There was a camera," he began, "a high-tech security surveillance camera on 2 World Financial Center—*this* very building. It was mounted two stories up to keep an eye on any activity that occurred on West Street." Chief Cassano's voice warmed up; his delight was obvious. "This was no ordinary camera. It could pan and zoom in. It had weather-resistant lenses and high-resolution focusing powers. It was built with night-vision capabilities. After all," he paused for effect, "this camera was made to stand guard and watch over an important piece of real estate, the Twin Towers!" He became serious again. "Now, this was a good camera, but the impact of the South Tower's collapse knocked it off its pedestal. It was upside down, literally hanging by its cables and pointing toward Liberty Street along West Street. Originally, we'd thought it had been rendered useless. But by some miracle, it was still functioning and recording."

Chief Cassano looked out over the crowd with pride and confidence in his eyes.

"I promised this distinguished audience that we would resolve whether the Magnificent Sighting on West Street ever took place, and so we shall." He signaled to his projectionist again. "Taken from the archives of the surveillance photos of 2 World Financial Center, we submit to you the following recording."

The room darkened again, and an image appeared on the screen. At first it didn't seem to be anything but static, a hazy, grainy picture with white splatter spots and some yellow lines barely visible.

"Yes, yes, we know it doesn't look like much to the naked eye," Chief Cassano said. "But with the forensics technology available, we filtered the images and distilled the pixels in this section here."

He gestured with his red laser again. The left edge of the grainy photo became the back view of a tall firefighter wearing a white chief's helmet. The letters on the tail portion of his fire jacket were clear, "First Deputy Commissioner William Feehan." Based on the shape of his jacket, it was clear he was standing erect and tall with his elbow bent as if he was saluting. The invited guests down below in front of the auditorium stage had begun to fidget about like children who were afraid of having a ghost story thrust upon them. There was also now movement on stage behind the green curtains. Rows of black footwear could be seen from under the green curtain's edge on both sides.

Chief Cassano continued, "And when we apply the same technical know-how to the rest of the image, we can see that—without a doubt, without a *trace* of doubt—what is happening here." His pointer outlined another fuzzy image on the screen. "We now know this to be—the late—Chief of Department—Peter Ganci!!"

Suddenly the blurry remaining portion of the picture transformed from disorganized pixels on the screen into Chief Ganci, standing tall in the middle of West Street inside a whirlpool of debris. His arm was raised in full military salute while his face beamed with the boyish smile for which he was known.

The auditorium exploded. Camera flashes began going off like fireworks amid the applause and cheers. A woman even released a high, joyous, and loud scream. Onstage the green curtains swung back to reveal two squads of the New York City Fire Department's Pipe and Drums. With slow, deliberate steps, they marched toward the front of the stage, playing a slow and haunting rendition of "Danny Boy." I stood as did all the high-ranking uniforms around me and saluted with tears of pride streaming down our faces. To me, the song is a message from those lost to us. It represents everything good in the American firefighter, a message that has been returned to the living. The secret I had kept inside had been released to the conscious world by my dream. The secret of the two highest ranking NYC Fire Chiefs turning to each other and executing a full blown military salute in their last seconds.

And for most it was time to celebrate. Waiters in purple topcoats appeared holding silver trays loaded with tall glasses of champagne.

But that was my cue: I held my salute for as long as humanly possible before staring to backpedal up the aisle to the glass doors. I could still hear "Danny Boy" ringing in my ears, but now it competed with the sound of champagne glasses breaking. The high-toned extravaganza had turned into a shanty, raucous funeral. There was sloppy singing and laughter. As I climbed up the sloped auditorium, I couldn't get it out of my head that Chief Ganci was smiling. I looked back down the aisle at them all, celebrating as if they'd found the Ark of the Covenant, the Holy Grail of 9/11. The fireworks-like flashbulbs, the silver trays of champagne, and the bagpipe music all started to blend together nightmarishly. The guests feasted and drank, but it had become bestial in some way. It was as if they were consuming our pride instead of honoring it.

I had to get out. Even above the din I could hear my heart beating as I reached the glass doors.

Fire Marshall Garcia yelled in my face, "Hey! Ten House, where the fuck you going? To play with your light?"

I took off running like a madman down the corridor toward the exit to West Street. Nothing could stop me as my mind kept pace with my feet. *This is not enough! This is not enough!* the words raced through my head as I kept running.

The fire marshal was yelling from behind me, "Hey, Ten House! You can't go out there; no one goes out there!"

I didn't care. I busted through the exit door to find a blinding white toxic fog.

I was back in my own dreamtime, my own nightmare reality. I was back on that morning in that dust and ash—although this time I was wearing my best dress uniform. Maybe the Australian bushmen know what this was like when they talk about dreamtime, about dreaming, and yet not dreaming, which is more real than much of our so-called reality.

For me, it was strange. It wasn't like I was dreaming anymore. It was as though I'd stepped into an alternate parallel universe.

Perhaps the first stages of death were surfacing within me. My breathing had become shallower. I was ankle-deep in debris and ash. I knew this place. I'd been here in my survivor nightmares. I'd reached a destination that was all too familiar to me. I was on West Street moments before the final pulverization of the North Tower. I could see to my far left the black billowy plumes of debris clouds expanding near the base. It was headed this way but slowed down like suspended animation to the frozen pace of dreamtime. A high-pitched sound permeated the dead air. The scarlet fiery plumes of fire were bearing down toward me. Fire trucks and emergency vehicles were tossed around like toys. All of it was headed ever so slowly in my direction.

Photo courtesy of Lauren X. Topelsohn

Then out of the toxic mist, I heard her voice. It came to me in triple deep echo from a distance.

"Daddy! Daddy, wait for me! Daddy!"

It was Tara. My tiny daughter was running to me through the

decimated landscape of pulverized ash and debris on West Street. Like some angelic mirage she hurried to my arms in her snow-white christening gown and cap, clutching her grandmother's ancient Irish Celtic cross.

"Da! Daddy, why didn't you wait for me?"

I was unable to hold back my tears; inside I must have really known that this was it. I stooped to hold her as only a father can.

"Daddy is with you always my brave little girl," I whispered to her softly.

"Why are we here, Da?" she asked so innocently and sweetly.

"I don't know, baby. Daddy doesn't know."

I could do no more than to tell her the truth, all the while clutching her and watching from over her shoulder as the death cloud expanded, getting closer and picking up speed. I lifted her up and, holding her tightly, headed down West Street. As we approached Liberty, something appeared in the distance ahead. It looked like some bulbous giant optical illusion, like a child's holiday snow globe. The aberration spun around in the middle of West Street, its top translucent, revealing the swirl of ash and office paper from the fallen South Tower. Inside, shadowy human figures stood erect and frozen in position.

"What is it, Daddy?" Tara yelled to be heard over the noise.

A loud, low humming was now emanating from the strange apparition.

"I think—I think I know, baby," I told her. "Don't be afraid. Just hold on to me!"

Holding Tara close with one arm, I dug in my pocket with my free hand for the little red flashlight. We got closer to the spinning apparition.

I yelled over the noise, "Hold on, baby!"

Summoning all our fortitude and courage, father and daughter entered the cone of the tornado. Tara and I found ourselves standing in the middle of a large space between the two chiefs who stood about twenty feet apart. They were presenting their final salutes to one other. Chief Feehan clearly struggled to keep his footing; his face was contorted with pain. Chief Ganci's eyes were closed; his face was set in a frown. The air was static but calm inside the vortex, the light a day-glow pale green emanating from the vortex's core. There was little time. As I held Tara close to me, papers swirled about us. Just outside the calm of the toxic tornado, a fire burst into life, ignited by the radiant heat of the approaching death cloud.

"Can they see us, Daddy?" Tara yelled.

"I think so. Maybe. Maybe for just a second!" I shouted my answer back in her ear.

I pointed my flashlight into Chief Feehan's face. He stood straighter now, and his face looked more relaxed. Tara held on to her cross with one hand and reached out to Chief Ganci with the other. To my utter surprise Chief Ganci's eyes were now wide open. He was smiling at *us*, actually beaming at us. I was certain he saw us. I then turned to Chief Feehan and found him standing tall and staring right at us with a big grandfatherly grin. His eyes shone, reflecting my flashlight. I barely had time to think.

"Thank you, Chief," I managed to say. "We will not forget you or Chief Ganci."

Outside of the twister, it was getting dark, closing in and capturing us as if God himself needed a picture—just one perfect snapshot image of how men at their best held up against the most evil that men are capable of. Lightning struck above, brilliant and loud etches of light, capturing images like God's own flashbulbs. Images appeared to us, were seen for a moment, and then gone: Sparky, the firehouse Dalmatian, standing his ground, growling, and snapping; a child tearing

Christmas wrapping paper to reveal a shiny red toy fire truck; a woman's hands reaching out to accept an American flag on behalf of a grateful nation; a young thirty-fifth president bellowing into a blistering silver microphone, "Ask not …!", even baby Tara's hands appeared holding the Double Star medal and Ribbon, two American soldiers exiting a helicopter, evacuating a mother and her child; and jet fighters in the missing-man formation harmonizing with the thunder and blending into the fading roll of the funnel lightning.

Tara and I were immersed in darkness. The great wind had died down. Tara buried her face into my chest, and I held her in both arms.

"Are they gone? Are they gone, Daddy?" she asked softly.

"Yes, baby, they're gone. They're all gone," I answered back, gently.

The two chiefs are gone along with hundreds of innocent civilians and hundreds of heroic firefighters and rescue workers, I thought to myself. The vacuum of the vortex must have ripped the red flashlight as well as Tara's cross from our hands. I placed Tara down on the ash-laden ground and took her hand, and we began to walk up toward the ruins, destination unknown.

I was grieving. We walked in the darkness for a couple of paces, holding hands and saying nothing until a ribbon of light appeared in the sky, allowing us to see each other's faces. It started to look like early dawn as Tara tugged at my hand to show me something behind us.

Just a few steps back where we had walked, a small bronze marker had somehow materialized in the middle of West Street. In the new light, I could read it, "On this stretch of highway from Vesey to Liberty Street during the attacks on the World Trade Center, September 11, 2001, brave men stood to the last minute outside the sixteen-acre hallowed ground to help rescue their fellow man. God rest their good souls."

Tara and I smiled at each other and continued walking. The pulverized gray ash, office papers, and occasional briefcase began to disappear. Even the mountainous piles of twisted girders and fiery debris somehow melted away before our eyes, and as we walked on, the ground turned into lush, green grass. As far as the eyes could see a great change was taking hold. In my mind, I could hear the classic Lennon/McCartney song "The Long and Winding Road." A bright hallelujah sun now shone in the sky above and dissipated the few remaining dark clouds as Sir Paul McCartney's voice opened up.

> ♪ "The long and winding road
> That leads to your door
> Will never disappear
> I've seen that road before.
> It always leads me here,
> Leads me to your door." ♪

Tara must have heard it, too, because she smiled at me. And just then the ground opened up on both sides of us. Huge square shapes appeared around us with what appeared to be refreshing bubbling waterfalls inside of them. Those represented the reflecting pools that memorialize the lost. Narrow walking paths snaked their way through the new grass, encircling newly hatched park benches, which in turn were shadowed and shaded by small green trees. Freedom Park, the great memorial, was sprouting up around us and brought to life by the hand of God.

Tara and I walked on. We watched in astonishment as a glass spike shot out from the earth before us. As it continued to rise, the sun that reflected from its glass top could no doubt be seen for miles. The Freedom Tower rose to its full height of 1,776 feet. The sound of birds singing reassured us that this park really did exist—and *would* exist in the real world, too. It comforted and reminded us. The deep boom of a foghorn suddenly split through the air, startling the birds aloft, and they began to circle the park. The navy's USS *New York* had just laid anchor in the harbor in front of Lady Liberty. Forged from the steel ruins of 9/11, the USS *New York* stood watch. Her metallic gray hull glistened in the waters of the harbor.

Tara and I turned around to find ourselves in front of a 9/11 museum, an archive of history and replete with relics of the human heroism from that fateful Tuesday morning.

Somewhere beyond the museum we heard a crowd. As Tara and I arrived on Broadway at the Canyon of Heroes, we saw red, white, and blue streamers flying along Church Street as every mother's son and daughter waved an American flag. The ticker tape parade was full-blown with proudly marching soldiers, camouflage-colored Humvees, Bradley armored fighting vehicles, jeeps, and tanks rolling along majestically. Somehow the troops had found their way home to us. Tara and I stood surrounded by color. *We are seeing history,* I thought. It was beautiful, and we were at peace. *We are honored.*

My final nightmare had taken on a mind of its own and now seemed to be rewarding me with a happy-ever-after ending. I didn't think it was possible to feel such joy while sleeping, and I knew I didn't want it to end. But the mood began to break, and I began to sweat. Tara tugged at my uniform sleeve.

"Daddy! Daddy!" she called urgently.

We were still watching the parade go by, but I bent down to hear what she was saying.

With her mouth next to my ear, she said loudly and plainly, "Mommy wants us home!"

And that was it: In a split second I was back in bed in our Brooklyn brownstone as the piercing sound of the security alarm system went off. Two very large African American fire department EMTs busted through the bedroom door.

"Start CPR!" I heard one say.

They dragged me off the bed, threw off my hat, loosened my tie, and threw a quick breath into me. The one with the dreadlocks started the resuscitator. I coughed a little and felt myself vomit.

I heard someone say, "He's breathing."

The alarm stopped. Someone had turned it off, and Annie, holding a sleeping Tara, walked by headed for Tara's bedroom.

I heard one of the EMTs call over to Annie, "He's gonna make it. You wouldn't believe this, lady, but this is the third one of these. In the last few weeks we've had three of these guys. These 9/11-ers need counseling."

I waited for Annie to say what she knew about this psychological pandemic of survivors or that she'd been aware of all my buried survivor guilt issues, but she didn't. Instead, she simply went back to check on Tara, who had slept through the whole event. In the quiet beside our daughter's bed, I heard her begin to pray and I pictured her with her head lowered, thanking God once again for keeping her husband alive. Instead of her usual Amen at the conclusion of the prayer, Annie exclaimed, "Christ, tell me the worst is over!"

The EMTs packed me up and took me away. I was in no condition to object, so I let them. The doctors assessed me at the emergency room, kept me overnight for observation, and released me the next morning. I came home with flowers, swearing to God, my wife, and my kid that I'd figured out the science of being a good parent and husband with a healthy mind, body, and spirit. I'd heard the closing words of Annie's prayer, and I wanted to reassure her that this was in fact the last crisis.

In the following days, I recorded in my journal what I remembered of what I have come to think of as my 9/11 death dream. The journal has long been collecting dust somewhere in our basement.

CHAPTER 13
Meeting and Saluting America's Mayor

After scaring my family silly—and embarrassing myself—I really had to straighten up. This last incident had changed something in me. My soul had been a war zone for those past months with my heart torn and conflicted between the raging guilt and all of the words I'd left unsaid. But that nearly fatal experience allowed me to fight through those conflicts. The tension I'd felt before was gone. And so to Annie's delight and my own, I became completely upright, a homebound Mr. Mom and the perfect Park Slope daddy.

I remained on my guard still. I couldn't risk a relapse, and so I concentrated on myself and focused only on my family. As an outlet for any remaining tension, I wrote about my 9/11 experiences and subsequent recuperation, an epic in itself.

These early stabs at self-expression yielded plenty. I authored a three-thousand-word essay, which I then did an audio recording of for the national StoryCorps project. David Isay, the founder of StoryCorps, had set up a field recording booth right in Manhattan's Grand Central Station. But when he read my essay, "The Magnificent Sighting on

West Street," he invited me to launch a new branch of the project, the StoryCorps booth at Ground Zero.

Isay has a mission. Starting in 2003, he began a ten-year project to record the tales of everyday people, stories that will inspire and enable the rest of us. These forty-minute recordings are then preserved for posterity at the American Folklife Center at the Library of Congress. In among the stories of survivors of the Great Depression and other combat veterans, of homemakers who recall life before modern conveniences, and of contemporary people making sense of the modern world is my story. It's one man's experience maybe but a miraculous story that presents the core of courage that I witnessed in two of my fellow firefighters.

Maybe this honor helped convince me that my story had value—and the importance of writing it. I'd already begun working with a writing group of other retired firefighters who would understand my vernacular and have a sense of my experiences. Together, those prompts began to give me some confidence in my writing, but it wasn't until the fifth anniversary of 9/11 that my creative, literary fuse was fully lit.

The events of the fifth anniversary were emotional as every 9/11 anniversary had been. There'd been some joyful moments. Seeing all of those international firefighters come to pay their respect filled me with pride. And there had been the tears, a salute we could all offer, as once again we heard those names read out.

But there had been some disappointments as well. President Bush never showed up at Ten House. Instead, we found out later that he had opted to have breakfast at another firehouse before making a brief appearance at Ground Zero to lay a wreath with the families.

I had a personal reason to regret his absence. Much to my Annie's dismay, I'd grown a wonderful full-blown mustache for the occasion. Annie had hated it from the start, and I'd promised to shave it at the end of the anniversary. As that old Confucius once said, "Man who argues with wife all day get no peace at night." And I was willing to give the mustache up soon. But just for that day, I thought I'd look regal like a proper firefighter! But, alas, there was no presidential visit for which to show it off.

But the day certainly had its moments. More important than any visiting dignitaries were the quieter times—the opportunity for reflection and prayer and the greetings and sincere handshakes from fellow firefighters. I've reunited with two of my own rescuers from September 11th on past anniversaries, and always have my eye out for them. It was a moist day and a solemn one. It was small wonder then that so many of us retreated to a nearby pub.

"Boy," said one survivor, "these anniversaries sure make me thirsty!"

He was speaking for many of us, but the gathering was joyful in its camaraderie. We talked; we sang. Our guests, the Brits, serenaded us. It had the makings for a long liquid evening. There was a little too much temptation for me in all this fun. I decided to head back to the Ten House to say good-bye to the brothers on duty before heading home.

The crowds were starting to thin. Even some of those who had the deepest ties to the Ten House were beginning to leave. As I approached the firehouse, I saw the fathers of Dennis Oberg, Jimmy Boyle, and Lee Ilepi. They had been firefighters, and I knew each man had loved the job. Each had raised a son to love it, too, and each had lost him. In times past, they'd all acted as fathers to me as well, consoling, briefing, and counseling me. Their words had made me feel that I could touch the sky while still keeping my feet firmly planted on the good earth. They didn't see me, and I didn't want to disturb their unique kinship. Instead, I watched them walk on by.

Firefighter George Bachmann at 10 House, with his "Hey Pal, every day is a gift" type of attitude.

I then entered the firehouse to look at some of the memorials the house had set up to those we had lost. The faces of my lost brothers, etched on plaques, sparked my own private picture show—a sort of a mental roll call: Lieutenant Gregg Atlas, a knowledgeable and gritty engine officer (we'd celebrated his twentieth anniversary just before the attack); Lieutenant Steve Harrell, an all-around musician and ladder officer, whose life is celebrated every year in an annual jam session; firefighter Jeff Olsen, an up-and-coming, aggressive member destined to become a fire officer; Paul Pansini, a respected firefighter was posthumously promoted to fire marshal; retired Captain James

Corrigan, head of fire and safety operations for the World Trade Center complex; and Shawn Tallon, a hero marine as well as a firefighter. All of those names—all those men—gone. I silently congratulated myself for getting myself into an emotional twist for the third time that day. It was hard, but I tried to compose myself.

Coffee helped even if it was just something to do. I walked away from those haunting memorials and made my way to the kitchen, where I poured myself a mug. Finally breathing normally again, I decided it was time to leave. I made a quick stop in the ground floor bathroom, and while I was washing my hands, I had what I thought was a flashback.

My name was being called over the intercom just as it had been that Tuesday morning, September 11, 2001. On that day, I'd been called up to the captain's office—and that's when we heard the first plane hit. But no, this time was different. This time my presence was requested out by the house watch area.

"Is retired firefighter George Bachmann in the firehouse?" the static voice asked. "If so please, report to the front, ASAP!"

When I got to the front, I didn't know what to think. Two young officers came up to me and began to give my uniform the once over, straightening my tie. One of them told me the mayor wanted to see me.

The mayor? I thought to myself. *Oh, I get it. Mayor Bloomberg wants a photo op and to meet a survivor or something. Ah well, it is part of the job, right?* So I donned my white gloves and let them lead me over to the firehouse by the front door. They raised it, and I saw small pockets of firefighters and officers. They were smiling, beaming at me as if someone was about to jump out and yell, "Happy Birthday!"

What happened instead was that a small group of suits who'd had their backs to me opened up. The small crowd parted like the Red Sea, only instead of Moses, a man with a subtle hunch in his gait, wearing glasses and a sharp suit, came briskly toward me with both of his hands out.

"Are you him?" he asked. "Are you the fireman who's writing about the two chiefs?"

He grabbed my hand.

"Yes. Yes, I am, Mayor Giuliani," I answered while shaking his hand nervously.

The honorable Mayor Rudolf Giuliani had decided to look up the fireman who was writing about his two favorite hero chiefs that perished on 9/11.

"I'm glad to meet you, your Honor. You've done some good psych work for me while I was home recuperating from my injuries."

I knew I sounded like a bumbling idiot, but I wanted to tell him how grateful I was. Still, he wasn't done with me.

"I came here to ask you something," he told me, smiling. Just then a photographer broke out of his entourage, and as he came closer, I was turned around. A quick flash and it was over. "Before I go I just wanted to ask you if it's true."

The former mayor was shaking my hand again this time to say good-bye. With all of the excitement, I had no idea what he was referring to. He spoke again, spelling it out.

"Is it true? Did they salute each other? Did you see them?"

I looked past his thick glasses and into his eyes. He really wanted to know. I thought for a second. I wanted to say something memorable, but I could only say what was in my heart.

"They are saluting still, your Honor," I said calmly.

The politician known as "America's Mayor" reared his head as his politician's smile gave way to a more solemn look as though something inside of him was now paying attention. With that, he walked back to the waiting entourage of bodyguards and accompanying suits.

By now a larger crowd of onlookers, including other firemen, had gathered, and the former mayor was about to join them and be engulfed once more in his protective circle. But Giuliani suddenly stopped short. I had no idea what he was about to do. He turned to face my direction, drew himself up to the position of attention, and then executed a long, slow full military salute. This set off a chain reaction of salutes from the surrounding firefighters, police officers, and civilians. I returned the salute and congratulated myself again for becoming emotional for the fourth time today.

This fifth anniversary is kickin' my ass, I thought to myself.

Retired Firefighter George Bachmann and former NYC Mayor Rudy Giuliani on the 5TH anniversary of 9/11, Ground Zero ceremonies.

I called Anne and told her I was on my way home. I figured I would fill her in on the day's events when I got back. I picked her up a glass 9/11 knickknack that lit up inside and bought Tara a teddy bear wearing a fireman's helmet. In the cab on the way back to Brooklyn, I found myself looking out the window and thinking. We were crossing the Brooklyn Bridge as the sun was beginning to set, and I found myself looking out at a city skyline that had been so damaged and changed in my lifetime—just as I had been injured and changed—not only by the evil of that day but also by the heroism that I had the privilege to witness.

My mind was racing, and I was hit by a realization. Short of selling my soul to the devil, I would give anything to tell the world about the saluting chiefs.

"Where was God that day, that awful morning?" had asked so many Americans in the weeks after 9/11. "Why didn't He intervene?"

Well, I couldn't pretend to know where God was on 9/11, but I knew where his fingerprints were. As a survivor, I believe that God's fingerprints were all over West Street. Unknown to me at the time, the first inkling of a calling was surfacing in my battered soul. I'd been trained and programmed as a combat soldier, a Vietnam veteran, and a New York City firefighter to never leave a good man behind. So many of them were gone now—but maybe I could bring them back by way of the written word to the American literary landscape. A cornucopia of insecurities made me think of something else instead. *I'm no wordsmith. I'm no Hemingway.* My negative side always seemed to get the last say on the subject.

Annie and sweetie pie Tara greeted me at the brownstone door. We made our sweet exchanges, kisses for gifts and more kisses all around.

"I've got dinner on the stove," Annie announced.

"I'm going downstairs for a second," I said. "I'll be right up."

Tara followed Mommy's shadow in the hall. I got to my makeshift basement office and took off my hat and tie. There were writing materials on the desk. I heard Tara tiptoe down the steps and knock gently at the door.

"Daddy, Mommy wants you to take off your uniform and come up for dinner," she said with that tiny voice.

"Okay, but only if I can get a hug," I replied.

As she came into my arms, I noticed that my little girl was wearing new cotton PJs. They were white with little characters on them: Dorothy and Toto from *The Wizard of Oz* followed closely behind by Scarecrow, Tin Man, and Lion.

"Tell Mommy I'll be right up," I said as we pecked each other with a little kiss.

Tara was attending one of the best parochial schools in Brooklyn. Her education was secure, thanks in part to the 9/11 Compensation Board. We were confident that we would soon be closing on a new house in Windsor Terrace, a neighborhood not too far away from Park Slope. Annie had become one of the staff nurses in the Fire Department's World Trade Center Medical Monitoring Program, which was dedicated to helping survivors and Ground Zero workers.

Even with Tara's reminder, my mind filled with the words of a famous writer, "The conscious dreamer moves in a circle to recapture the past." I picked up my pencil as if I might have the audacity to start an outline. As the lead tip of the pencil began moving across the blank sheet of paper, I could feel the strength of a battalion of men channeling into the writing utensil. As if once again in a trance, I had a last thought, *I am the son—of many—Fathers. It's always darkest before the dawn.*

Then the words just spilled out of me, and I began to write, In these few hours, in the hours before dawn, I walk these restless dreams alone....

"I am certain that after the dust of centuries have passed over our cities, we too, will be remembered not for the victories or defeats in battle or politics, but for our contribution to the human spirit."

JOHN F. KENNEDY (1917-1963)

Vice Presidential hopeful Governor Sarah Palin posing with the officers and firefighters of Ladder 10 and Engine 10 at Ground Zero in September 2008.

"Every delegate of the world should pass through the
Ten House and hear the heartbeat of history."

ACKNOWLEDGEMENTS

(Many Thanks) The author would like to acknowledge the following individuals that have either inspired or supported the creation of *Tara's Cross:*

I would like to thank President Obama for his inspiration and courage.

I would like to thank President George W. Bush for protecting me and my family and having the guts to go after the bad guys.

The vision of First Lady Laura Bush and the President in that windswept dusty pit at Ground Zero September 11, 2002 for the first anniversary, meeting and greeting the survivors and 9/11 families will stay with me for all time.

I'd like to thank the Holy Father, Pope Benedict XVI for his blessings at Ground Zero on April 20, 2008.

I'd like to thank New York Governor Patterson and New Jersey Governor Corzine for visiting Ten House on September 11, 2008.

I'd like to thank Homeland Security Director Michael Chernoff for visiting Ten House on September 11, 2008.

I'd like to thank the lovely and vivacious Alaskan Governor Sarah Palin for her photo op with the Ten House in September 2008.

I'd like to thank Honorable Mayor Rudolph Giuliani for his words of courage and inspiration on the days and months following the September 11th attacks. He is truly America's Mayor.

I'd like to thank NYC Mayor Bloomberg for rebuilding our Ten House firehouse after the attacks, and replacing our fire trucks.

I would like to thank NYC Fire Commissioner Nicholas Scopetta, Chief of Department Sal Cassano, Fire Marshall Luis Garcia, Malachy Corrigan, and all staff at Fire Department Counseling Unit.

I would like to thank the 9/11 families, the men and women of our armed forces, and all Ground Zero rescue and recovery units, Ground Zero workers, and their support groups.

I would like to thank Barbara Simmons of the Brooklyn VA, and the Vietnam Veterans of America.

Many thanks to Lauren X. Topelsohn, Esq, for your picture, you'll always be my 9/11 sister.

Also, Nella Dyn for her editing skills, Maria Carrion, and Janet Hamlin for her illustrations.

Many thanks for the back cover photo of the author to Nikibi Studio on Seventh Avenue in Park Slope, Brooklyn, NY

Many Thanks to Firefighter John Marabito and the members and officers past and present of Ladder 10 and Engine 10, the Ten House.

Many thanks to Firefighter Peter D'Ancona and his wife Barbara along with the Fire Department Motorcycle Club for raising funds for the in-house memorial for our fallen brothers.

Thanks to Sam Kedem, counselor for WTC permanency project. As well as Susanna Miller Pence LCSW for giving me direction.

Thanks to principal Mr. James Flanagan and all teachers and parents of St. Saviour Elementary School in Brooklyn, members of McFadden Bros. American Legion Post #1380 in Brooklyn, bartenders and patrons of Farrell's Bar and Grill in Brooklyn.

Special thanks to Thomas Tobin Sr. and Bridie Boland Tobin and the entire Tobin family for all the love and support, and little Wee T too, we love you all.

Thanks to The Beatles for all their songs.

Finally to my wife, thanks for helping me make this memoir, and for not hitting me in the head with a rolling pin, during my struggle to make this book. I will love you for one eternity.

To my Tara, Daddy could not have healed without you. You will always and forever be my little girl. I will love you for one infinity.

Breinigsville, PA USA
02 December 2009
228455BV00001B/1/P